The Way of Whisky

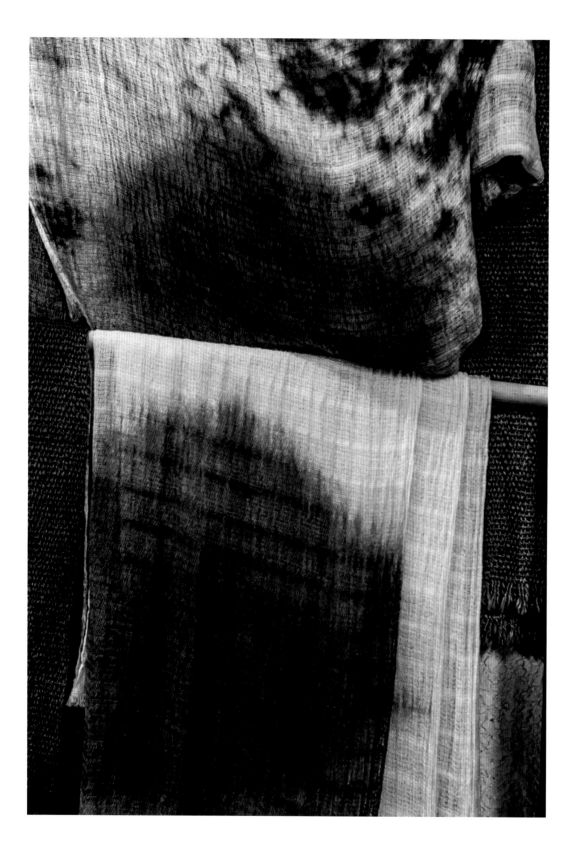

The Way of Whisky

A journey around Japanese whisky

Dave Broom
Photography by Kohei Take

Mitchell Beazley

ウイスキー道

An Hachette UK Company
www.hachette.co.uk

First published in Great Britain in 2017 by Mitchell Beazley,
a division of Octopus Publishing Group Ltd
Carmelite House
50 Victoria Embankment
London EC4Y 0DZ
www.octopusbooks.co.uk

Distributed in the US by
Hachette Book Group
1290 Avenue of the Americas
4th and 5th Floors
New York, NY 10104

Distributed in Canada by
Canadian Manda Group
664 Annette St.
Toronto, Ontario, Canada M6S 2C8

ISBN 9 781 78472 142 8

A CIP catalogue record for this book is available from the British Library.

Printed and bound in China

10 9 8 7 6 5 4 3 2 1

Publisher Denise Bates
Art Director Juliette Norsworthy
Senior Editor Alex Stetter
Copy Editor Margaret Rand
Proofreader Jamie Ambrose
Indexer Hilary Bird
Design Praline (Giovanni Pamio and David Tanguy)
Photography Kohei Take
Senior Production Manager Katherine Hockley

CONTENTS

It's been a long journey.

Introduction

This is how my first-ever day in Japan went. Arrive at Tokyo's Narita airport, sushi for lunch in the city, bullet train (*shinkansen*) to Kyoto, train to Yamazaki. Before I quite knew what was happening, I was sitting alongside my old friend and mentor Michael Jackson while chief blender Seiichi Koshimizu was asking us to taste Suntory's whisky. It was reddish in colour and had an aroma unlike anything we had encountered before. We hazarded guesses. He smiled his shy smile. 'It is *mizunara*. Japanese oak. We say it smells of temples.'

As I said, it was my first day in Japan. I hadn't had a chance to smell a temple. Now I wanted to. It was a lesson in the cultural aspect of aromas. Smell is not fixed by language, but open to interpretation and that interpretation is partly determined by upbringing. I might say that the smell of a smoky whisky is like the Glasgow underground *c.*1967. A Japanese colleague might interpret it as a specific medicine. Past and place dictate the terms we use to describe the smells around us. Part of the fascination of travel is discovering new tastes and flavours, comparing home with this new place. Later that evening I was sitting next to a *maiko* (Kyoto dialect for geisha). 'Do you eat many small potatoes in Scotland?' was her opening line.

This *mizunara* was different, though. It was resinous, slightly like sandalwood, with a little bit of coconut; but none of these terms are quite accurate. I could have mentally labelled it 'exotic' and moved on, but it had me. I was being led by the nose deeper into Japan. 'It smells of temples' was now a suggestion that I should seek out these places and inhale them. In time, that led me to learn about incense, an aromatic thread which led from Japan, to Vietnam, to Arabia, high-end perfumers, and back to Japan again.

Mizunara, I realized, slowly, was a way of creating a marker for (some) Japanese whisky. Its use said: 'This aroma is one way in which our whisky is special. We use it because of its aroma and that aroma means something special to us.' It rooted the whisky in Japan, it helped to define it as different.

On that same day, Suntory's Mas Minabi described Japanese whisky as being 'transparent'. These whiskies had an aromatic intensity unlike Scotch; they were paradoxically managing to be vivid yet delicate, subtly powerful. The flavours were ordered, complex and seamless on the tongue; they had a clarity and precision. Some were familiar from Scotch, but the manner in which they presented themselves was different. Each glass was whisky, but it was not the whisky I had been brought up on. What makes Japanese whisky 'Japanese' has obsessed me ever since.

I was lucky enough to begin travelling to the country twice, sometime three times, a year. Every time I returned, another door seemed to open. I thought initially it was because I was beginning to be trusted, but that was just ego at work. I suspect that answers to the questions would have been given if I had known what questions to ask. I was being tutored, but was too stupid to realize it. Those apparently opaque, philosophical answers were in fact perfectly rational when my mind caught up. And so it continued, slowly moving forward, still asking that question: 'But how is it Japanese?'

Part of the answer lay in the often subtle differences in production between Japanese and Scottish distillers. Some of it came from the climate and the way it influenced maturation. There was *mizunara,* of course, but not every whisky contained it. The rest of the conundrum, I began to believe, was rooted in place. Whisky does not sit apart from the culture that produces it. So much impacts on its making: ingredients, climate, landscape, cuisine, palate, manner of consumption. The cultural terroir in Japan will be different to that in Scotland – or in any other whisky-making nation.

What if, I began to wonder, there was some unseen link between Japan's whisky-makers and the country's other traditional craftsmen? The more I visited and talked to whisky-makers the more I saw that they were *shokunin*, master artisans dedicated to their craft. The way they approached whisky was imbued with the concept of *kaizen* – continuous incremental improvement. There seemed to be an aesthetic behind it that linked whisky to a web of other crafts: cooking, ceramics, metalwork, wood-work, and also design and architecture; even the way bartenders went about their craft. The more I looked, or obsessed about it, the more I saw the same impulse. That clarity was in the food, in the lack of ornamentation; it was there in *haiku*. Equally, maybe I was making connections where there were none. Maybe they just made whisky. Perhaps I was just mad. I had to find out one way or other.

So back I went, to visit all the distilleries and see other craftspeople. Ask them what motivated them, what lay behind their work. See if those connections were in fact there. A road test in both senses. A book at the end of it no matter what, but not one just of tasting notes, scores, sections on history and how whisky is made, and in-depth facts and figures. All of that is useful, and other writers will give you that.

I wanted to try and find out why whisky matters, what drives these people on, how it links to that wider culture, where tradition comes in. How strong was their craft, or how precarious?

The great 21st-century paradox is how greater connectivity has allowed us to separate ourselves from those things we are told we don't like. We no longer browse. Algorithms tell us what, even who, we like. Something like whisky is reduced to little more than tasting notes and statistics about process. The richness and messiness of this complex, interdependent world are being steadily eroded, the connections are being lost and with their passing whisky floats free of place, history, weather, water and rock, and the people who make it. Separating whisky from all these things diminishes it and diminishes the people who make it. It can't be allowed to happen.

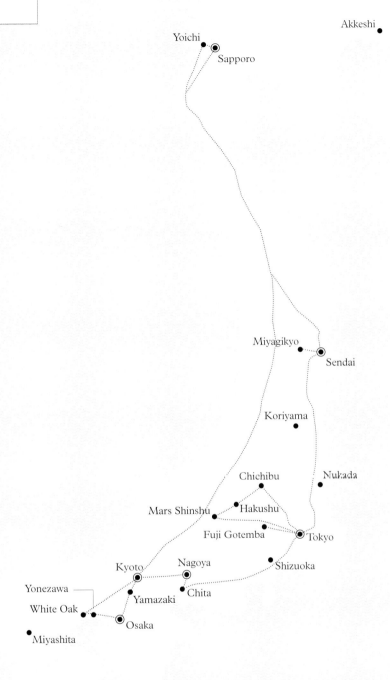

JAPAN

● Distilleries

◉ Main Cities

Akkeshi

Yoichi
Sapporo

Miyagikyo
Sendai

Koriyama

Nukada

Chichibu
Mars Shinshu Hakushu
Fuji Gotemba Tokyo
Kyoto Nagoya Shizuoka
Yonezawa Chita
White Oak Yamazaki
Osaka
Hiroshima Miyashita

Fukuoka

Hombo Tsunuki

Tokyo

The route is by now familiar. Flight to Tokyo Haneda, monorail to Hamamatsucho, taxi to the hotel, through the back streets, under the tracks, past tiny restaurants and apartment blocks, half-hidden shrines next to car parks, glimpses of walled-in river. People everywhere. Tokyo is in a constant sense of seethe. My head is still blurry from 12 hours on the plane.

My destination is Shiodome, a sleek, anonymous district of razor-edged multistorey office blocks. The only nod to frivolity is the enormous clock, designed by Hayao Miyazaki, which seems to have been beamed in from his film *Howl's Moving Castle* and yet – and this is very Tokyo – you are only a ten-minute walk from Ginza, 20 minutes from the sushi bars around Tsukiji fish market, while the wonderful chaos of Shimbashi is a five-minute stroll.

Tokyo is a series of islands, and to stretch the metaphor to breaking point, my desert island is the Park Hotel, which after many years is now more a home than a hotel. It has amazing bar staff, contemporary art exhibitions (each floor has been decorated by a different artist), while from one side there is a view over Tokyo Tower to Mount Fuji. Not today, though. It's rainy season.

Check in, then back down to reception for my first meeting with Kohei Take. We needed a unified look for this mad book project and that meant only using one photographer. Question was, who? I knew no Japanese snappers. Thankfully my friend Alice knew Alicia Kirby, who used to work for *Monocle* magazine in Japan and was, according to Alice, 'the best-connected person I know'. One email later Alicia had given me three names. Take's images were the best, so he was hired.

He comes in, shaved head, scarf, denim jacket, a ball of energy and good humour. I like him immediately. I try to articulate what the idea is – people, craftsmanship, artisans, tradition, landscape – and whisky. Not cliché picture-postcard Japan but real Japan, images that link the whisky to the land, the people, and perhaps establish that net of connection between them all. 'I get you,' he says. 'Eyes, hands, work, water. This will be fun. Now, get some rest. I'll meet you at 7.30 and we can go and get the bus to Gotemba.' Ah, the romance of the whisky-writer's life. I avoid the bar and head up to the room. I know I'll wake at 3am. It's a weird fact about jet lag. No matter what time zone you've come to that internal alarm clock is triggered at 3am. Weird, huh?

Tokyo: a vast, dazzling, baffling metropolis.

Fuji-Gotemba

富士御殿場蒸溜所

Tokyo to Gotemba

Up at dawn, clouds lifting over Tokyo, gilding Shiodome's towers. Blue skies after the grey of yesterday, though Fuji remains hidden. A quick breakfast – miso soup, salmon, rice, pickles, pasta, green tea. Bulk up as it's a long day – with whisky involved.

The city is waking up. Schoolchildren in matching white hats tiptoe out of the subway like mice venturing across a carpet. The sun seems to drain the colour from everything. Tokyo in the daytime becomes monochrome, its range of muted greys matched by the salarymen's trousers – the switch from identikit black a concession to summer's start. Ties have been abandoned, along with jackets. Short sleeves are apparently mandatory. Women are permitted pastel shades. There's the occasional frilly parasol. People walk at a purposeful angle, ten degrees from the vertical.

Tickets bought, we stand in the sun waiting for the 08.20 to Gotemba. The heat is rising. The rest of the passengers are on their way to raid Hakome's outlet stores. We head out onto the elevated highway, glancing in at office windows, trailing wires and, as the city begins to loosen its grip, a cluster of brightly lit love hotels promising total discretion while at the same time yelling 'HAVE SECRET SEX HERE!!!'

The road curves into forest, trees swagged in vines, shooting us through tunnels and into a valley mirrored with rice paddies. Ahead, above a mountain ridge, above the clouds and impossibly high, starched with snow, floating, is Fuji-san.

I climbed it a few years back and blended whisky on the summit to commemorate the 15th anniversary of the Scotch Malt Whisky Society in Japan. I remember a long zigzag through dust and boiled lilac-and-red rock dusted with sulphur, looking like a giant's breakfast cereal, to a bunkhouse where we tried to sleep; rising at 2am to shuffle to the summit in time for the first golden rays to light up every edge of rock, every smile and crease on the tired, happy faces.

Fuji, as the artist Hokusai showed, is always there. His series of prints, *36 Views of Mount Fuji*, captures its constant presence: hidden in the corner of the frame, peeking from behind a roof, almost obscured on a building site; in the centre of a huge, half-made barrel; blood-red in the sunset, framed in a great wave. Fuji-san walks across Japan. Even the cloud sitting where it should be takes on significance.

We're the only people getting off at Gotemba. We grab a taxi and head uphill, through cable-draped streets, past manicured trees, quiet gardeners and dog-walkers, to the distillery: startlingly huge, red-brick. Behind, only 12km (7½ miles) away, Fuji remains behind its veil.

A quick prayer and the trip starts.

FUJI-GOTEMBA

I'm here to meet with Kirin's master blender, Jota Tanaka. Tall, with the air of an ascetic, he is a witty, ever-eager figure, keen not just to show his own distillery, but to find out what else is happening around the whisky world. He is one of my touchstones and someone who, over the following months, helps to unfold more layers. 'Don't call me Tanaka-san,' he says. 'I'm Jota.'

Fuji-Gotemba distillery was built in the era of optimism, when Japan was sucking down as much whisky as it could – and exporting none. The Canadian-based giant Seagram had already spread into Scotland (it had owned Chivas Bros since the 1950s), as well as owning a significant number of rum distilleries in the Caribbean and South America. Now it was looking east. With Japanese brewer Kirin as equal partner, the distillery was built in 1972 and began running the year after.

It made sense. Japan's economy was booming, and whisky, then as always as a signifier of success, was keeping pace. Industrious and hardworking by day, after work the country's salarymen could indulge in tie-loosening relaxation with a *mizuwari* (whisky, ice and water) or ten. For a distiller with global ambitions, Japan was a no-brainer.

Building close to Fuji had a certain symbolism – and also optimism. This, after all, is an active volcano, while there's the not insignificant matter of the Japan Self-Defense Force's (live) firing range close by. Lava and shells. Neither mix particularly well with alcohol.

There were more practical reasons, as Jota explained. 'People from the firms searched all round Japan and narrowed it down to eight potential sites. This was chosen for its location – the highway had been built – and climate. The average temperature is 13°C (55.4°F), the humidity is 85 per cent. It's good for ageing whisky – but not for people!'

There was also plentiful volcanic-rock-filtered water from the mountain. It takes 51 years for the melted snow to pass through the bedrock to one of the distillery's three 100m-deep (328-foot) wells.

To most visitors, Japanese distilleries are a simulacra of Scottish ones. The ingredients are the same, so is the kit.

Most also make more than one style. Though, like Scotch, Japanese whisky's fortunes were built on blends, unlike Scotland its distillers have never exchanged stock, forcing them to make all of their blending requirements in-house. This is one of the roots of the whisky industry's relentless innovation, driven by a constant need to widen that palette of flavours. None of this would have bothered Seagram. After all, this is how the Canadian industry had evolved – base spirit made from corn, then flavouring whiskies made with other 'small grains', all aged separately, and then blended.

To get to grips with Gotemba you first have to put thoughts of malt whisky to one side. Here, it all starts with grain whiskies. We wander past the fermenters (the fact that the grain fermenters outnumber malt fermenters by 12 to eight underlines what the dominant style is) and into an amazing control room whose original 1970s kit gives it the air of a Bond villain's lair. 'It was cutting-edge 40 years ago!' laughs Jota, as we walk into the surprisingly small grain stillhouse.

There are three still-types working here and, judging by the heat and hiss, doing so simultaneously. There's a bourbon-style setup where a rye-rich mash is put through beer column and doubler producing a heavy type of distillate at 70% ABV. There's also a 'kettle and column' setup similar to one I'd seen at Gimli (a former Seagram distillery near Winnipeg, now owned by Diageo). After being run through the beer column, 50,000

The distillery was built in 1972.

Long fermenting is the norm here.

litres of the corn and malted-barley distillate are collected in the 'kettle', reheated and driven through a 61-plate rectifier. It might be high strength but it is packed with flavour, giving Gotemba its medium-weight style. A third set of five columns produces a corn-based distillate which, though the same strength as the kettle and column, is lighter in character, thanks to a more highly selective process. Stir in different yeast types and cask types and there is a huge range of possibilities just on the grain side.

Column-still whisky is often dismissed as being little more than neutral packing. Gotemba's approach shows that it is a flavour-led contributor to a blend's character. It would be fair to say that in Scotch whisky grain is the lighter partner in the blend; it may give flavour and texture and add character, but the malts are what give the power. Gotemba reverses this. Its malt is the light, estery, delicate component, the grain – especially those heavy and medium variants – gives the heft.

Why this reversing of the norm? 'Scotch was famous for robust, masculine malt, therefore grain had to be lighter in flavour. Our malt is almost feminine, so we saw an opportunity to use a diverse range of grain whiskies as key drivers.'

Everything in the malt production is there to help lighten its nature: long fermentation, for example, and distillation in pot stills with upward-slanting lyne arms (said to be modelled on those at Strathisla, but looking more like Glen Keith's), which make any heavy components turn from vapour back to liquid and fall exhausted into the roiling mass below to be redistilled.

Jota and his team are also experimenting with different yeast strains – and here's another difference to the approach of Scotch where one style of yeast is used. In Japan, as in some Canadian and US distilleries, yeast is a vital contributor to flavour. The Kirin-owned Four Roses, also an ex-Seagram plant, perhaps takes this to its extreme with five different strains being used.

'I never thought of yeast in whisky until I went to work at Four Roses,' says Jota. 'Now I am fascinated by it. We used two from the start: one fruity, one for body. Now we are trying others for the malt, including ale yeast. We'll use a different yeast for each of the grain styles as well.'

We stroll to the warehouse, a single space, 23 racks high and 23 casks deep on each side. Its scale dwarfs and disorientates; you lose your sense of perspective as the cliffs of oak rise on either side and into the distance.

It wasn't built in this way for its aesthetics, but for practical reasons. 'We were limited for space, so the warehouses had to be taller than normal,' Jota explains. 'At the same time we didn't want the same effect as you get in Kentucky of temperature extremes between different floors. We wanted smooth ageing, so we decided not to divide it up into floors but to leave it as an open space.'

That said, there is still a temperature difference between bottom and top and as that impacts on flavour – the hotter, the more extract from the wood – Jota blends each batch from every layer of the warehouse.

While most is aged in ex-bourbon casks there is some new wood, especially for that heavy grain, and a recent widening of choice into sherry – PX, Oloroso – and *mizunara*.

We're back in the blending lab, samples littering the table, talking seasons, maturation peaks, and the role of the Japanese palate in the creation of a style. 'Our first master blender, Ichiro Ogino, wanted something that is smooth and mellow, a whisky which appealed to Japanese consumers,' Jota explains. 'In Japan, in general, aficionados love smoky Islay whiskies, but most people find [that style] hard and tend to like grain-style whiskies, so ours have been based around the medium and light grains – not robust but balanced and smooth. Don't get me wrong; we don't want to make something which is light in flavour!' Hence the need for a spectrum of flavours and weights within the grain components.

A control panel straight from a Bond movie.

富士御殿場蒸溜所

富士御殿場蒸溜所

The pot stills make a delicate style (opposite). The compressed space of the grain plant (above). A complex array of flavours are produced here (above right).

When mature, the light type is fresh, citric, slightly hay-like and, thanks to the char on the casks, with a smoky pine-needle element. Sweet and fine in structure, it adds subtlety to a blend.

The medium grain from the kettle and column is sweet also, but has a more mellow note with some caramel, toffee and light citrus. Texturally it's unctuous with some fresh melon and a flavour akin to raspberry sauce on vanilla ice cream, before some treacle toffee hits on the back palate. It's remarkable.

The heavy grain, when mature, is aromatically powerful, with heavy rose petal, jasmine and berry fruits with a whisper of mint chocolate and black cherries in the distance. The rye adds spice and a slight astringency along with menthol. It's bold, it's big and you can see how a small percentage would go a long way in a blend.

The malt, the icing on the cake, is floral, with kiwi, William pear and fresh strawberry. Jota then brings out a lightly peated variant. Hang on, smoke? I'm sure smoke hadn't been mentioned. But why not? It's that principle of maximizing variety within a distillery style again. The smoke is very subtle, more a memory than a bold statement that brings to mind the aroma of a distant garden bonfire wisping down the street. There's also some of the piney, minty element in a few of the whiskies – maybe distillate-driven, maybe cask and climate. All, however, have an element of concentration to them. Layered, elegant, sometimes discreet, sometimes more forceful but always – this is Japan after all – polite.

There are only three bottled releases at the moment. Japan's decades-long whisky boom came to a juddering halt in the 1990s, when a combination of a new tax regime and a turning-away by a new generation from their fathers' drink saw sales plummet, and distilleries either close or go on very short-term working.

The industry might now have a global following, while domestic sales have returned to growth, but there isn't sufficient mature stock to satisfy this sudden rise in demand. Whisky-makers will always to some extent be playing a guessing game—predicting what a fickle public might wish to drink in a decade's time. The Gotemba stocks, like those at all Japanese distilleries, have more holes than an absent-minded professor's sweater.

This presents either a challenge or an opportunity for Jota. He needs to maintain a presence, showcase the distillery's range, while having a less-than-complete selection to play with. This has meant small-scale releases of aged products—at the time of writing a 17-year-old malt and 25-year-old grain—and a greater emphasis on a flavour-led blend with No Age Statement, Fuji-Sanroku.

Removing an age statement not only makes sense in terms of allowing Jota access to the widest range of stock possible, but it also gives him as a blender fuller rein than having to wait for, say, 12 years for a whisky to mature.

It's an approach taken by all the Japanese distillers but has been met with a certain degree of how shall I put this? resistance from a whisky-drinking public brought up on the mistaken belief that age is a determinant of quality.

Jota's way of explaining the creative advantages of No Age Statement (NAS) whiskies is to point out that the character and quality of each whisky type, each cask in fact, doesn't move in a steadily rising line from 'poor' (immature) to 'excellent' (mature) but in an arc of possibilities. The whisky starts with sharply aggressive, immature elements, but as cask, spirit, air and time all impact, so it changes, rising through stages of maturity, flavours altering, eventually hitting a peak before the cask begins to exert greater control and the whisky becomes woodier.

Each style has its own arc, each cask type as well. Each tier within the warehouse will also create a different curve of flavour. Time therefore becomes a crude way of measuring quality. Maturity becomes a three-dimensional world of flavours from which a blender can select.

'It's to do with esters and how they change in maturation,' he explains. 'Green, pungent and sharp at the start; fruity, floral, round and mellow at the peak; and sour, woody and hard when it has gone over.' There is peak maturity, but it is dependent on mash bill, distillation technique, cask type and warehouse position.

'We have a way of describing this in seasonal food,' he goes on. '*Hashiri* is the freshest, the first; *shun* is the peak and *nagori* is the season coming to an end. Through the season, the taste of the food changes, but it makes the same shape as the maturation curve.' (See page 32.)

It was the first example of what would become a common theme, not just in terms of an explanation of maturity and No Age Statement whiskies, but the manner in which Japan's whisky-makers switch effortlessly from the technical world to the philosophical, because talking about

富士御殿場蒸溜所

whisky is the same as talking about food, and bringing in the Japanese approach to seasonality helps to root the whisky within a wider cultural and flavour-led framework.

This doesn't necessarily make the whisky taste different – though the close allying of whisky and food is of more concern in Japan than in any other whisky-making country – but it does I think show the mindset of the blender.

Jota is also bottling at higher strength, 50% ABV for Fuji Sanroku 'to increase the umami element' (see page 127) and the new blend has more of the heavy grain coming through, adding some structure and greater complexity and layering.

There's a further element here, which goes to the heart of the Japanese approach. It revolves around the moment of possession, the point when a distillery, set up in a Canadian fashion, began to make identifiably Japanese whisky. Any culture appropriates and absorbs external influences; all Japanese crafts came to the country via China or Korea, its whisky-making from Scotland, and in this case North America, but all have been transformed and continually refined, so that after a period of incubation they emerge familiar, but somehow different.

'We imported the know-how and equipment of Scotland, Canada and the US and tried to make something authentic,' Jota says. 'But we have tweaked it and made our own unique style by blending all these elements but also not being restricted by them and trying out something new. It's not Scottish malt or Canadian corn, or American bourbon. It is ours.' He pauses. 'Fuji-Sanroku sees some elements of different styles and compo-

For Jota Tanaka, peak maturity and umami are key to quality.

Bubble caps inside the column still (above) help produce a range of flavours for Gotemba's grain whiskies (above right).

nents, but it is still progressing. There is still room for improvement.' In that statement, another theme emerged – the *kaizen* approach, the constant moving forward, the refusal to accept that the template is fixed. For Jota this means gently adding weightier distillates to his palette – a burly 50:50 corn:barley mashbill, for example.

'There is a fine line between everything which can be done and what we try to do. We try to do a lot of things, but we don't show them all! In some countries they try everything and then bottle it. We want to challenge ourselves to create a new range of flavours which add value to what we have established.' In other words, there is focus within the experimentation.

We prepare to leave for Tokyo. Fuji Gotemba, it strikes me, is a little like the mountain: hidden in plain sight. A large distillery, an innovative one, yet one that has been quiet – too quiet I'd argue – about its achievements. There are stock issues, but there has also been a strange aversion to export. Even in Japan it has not been top of people's minds. It deserves to be better known, not just for the quality of its whiskies but the way in which its approach offers another facet of Japanese whisky.

I sense that something has shifted. There's a discreet boldness to Fuji Gotemba's whiskies and its new confidence.

Like *haiku* poet Issa's gastropod, it is on the move.

little snail
inch by inch
climb mount fuji!

TASTING NOTES

Fuji-Gotemba is steadily building
its reputation.

The stock shortage has meant that Jota Tanaka and team have had to be creative about releases. They have to build the brand, and as they gear up for export show as wide a range of styles and possibilities as possible. Limited releases, some only at the distillery, represent one way, while the innovative (but sadly limited edition) 'Housky' blending kit, with its two malts (light style and peated) and two grains (heavy and the kettle and column batch) plus glass and cans of soda, allows you to blend a Highball to suit your tastes.

At the time of writing there are three bottled products in wider distribution. The **Fuji-Gotemba 17-year-old single malt** (46% ABV) is made predominantly from the unpeated style, but there is a judicious splash of lightly peated make which gives a very subtle smokiness that is really only perceptible on the finish.

The nose is slightly oaky – this is a light whisky after all – with an oily, sappy, and almost peppery impact. The mintiness I often pick up in Gotemba is there as well, and in this expression moves the aroma into peppermint. It's intense and concentrated, but while there is a sense of age (the oldest whiskies in here are 19 years old) it also has real clarity.

Its companion, **Fuji-Gotemba 25-year-old Small Batch Grain** (46% ABV) is a blend of the heavy and batch grains aged for between 25 and 30 years. This opens with some oak, but it's less obvious than on the malt – remember, the Gotemba grains are heavier in character. Fruits are to the fore with grilled pineapple, apple, then more estery top notes like pear drop, even acetone. A heavier toffee-like sweetness keeps it from becoming too flighty, and with water a waxiness develops. It's tightly structured and concentrated on the tongue with flavours of baked fruits (with their sticky syrups), crème brûlée and a touch of sandalwood. Things lighten with water into poached pears, a little clove and that menthol note. (For the Fuji-Sanroku blend, see page 179.)

Gotemba to Tokyo

And with that we head out, the clouds gathering gravid with rain, the mountain a figment. Take and I wander behind the office block along a winding path to a grove of trees. Stone foxes glare at me from the entrance to a small Shinto shrine.

That night Jota and I head into the back streets of Shimbashi for dinner. Next to Shiodome, it is a remnant of an older Tokyo, the grubby hem to Ginza's mescalin glitter. Compressed around the mainline station is a chaotic jumble of streets crowded with pubs, bars and *izakayas*. In daytime it is quiet and drab, at night a carnival of loud, laughing office workers, street musicians, panhandling hippies, outside tables, the feel of smoky chicken fat glossing your face.

We duck into an *izakaya* and head up the steep stairs to a tiny room where laughter roars like breakers on a reef. 'Welcome to whisky reality!' Jota calls as we concertina ourselves around a tiny table. Highballs appear immediately. Around us in the fug of smoke are hot-faced, white-shirted men, glasses full, all complaining about their bosses and bellowing with laugh-ter. Every table is littered with half-forgotten food. More Highballs appear.

Izakayas are the bedrock upon which whisky was built – and foundered. They are Japan's dive bars, but with better food: places where office politics and stress are forgotten for a few hours, where glasses clink and whisky and beer are supped. Their noise and boisterous nature are the opposite of what visitors expect and are taught about – the hushed sushi bar, the calm of a *ryokan*.

Izakayas are vital in both senses of the word, offering a much-needed release valve and in a life-affirming, high-spirited fashion. In the West we have been brought up to believe that Japanese whisky is all about high-end blends and fine single malts. It is, but Jota is correc: this is the reality. The industry needs *izakayas*, it needs volume, it needs to balance contemplation with exuberant behaviour.

Izakayas – Japan's decompression chambers

SEASONS

Jota re-emerged later in the week when we went to the Minkaen folk house museum in Kawasaki to try our hand at indigo dyeing. His original plan was for us to sit *zazen* (Zen meditation) in his home town of Kamakura, but 'the hydrangeas are in flower, and it's really busy'. It's not just cherry blossom, you know. Wafting our newly dyed garments he, Take and I walk through the collection of old houses which constitute the museum. It's a remarkable snapshot of how quickly Japan has changed. Many of these wooden, thatched buildings were lived in until relatively recently. Inside them is the scent of *hinoki* wood and woodsmoke from the central firepit. They are places of space and shadows, diffused light and a world where function could be changed simply by the drawing of a screen.

We sit down for a lunch of soba (buckwheat noodles), and talk again of the seasonality of flavour, and how from a Japanese sensibility, seasons do not shift dramatically but are tiny moments of incremental change, each with its own personality. 'Each,' says Jota, 'has its own *hashiri*, *shun* and *nagori*.'

It is an approach that tells you to be aware of the impulse of change, feel the wind in your face, the evanescent smells as flowers begin to open, the moment when the fish reach the right size; learn the best moment to try something, comprehend flavour and aroma and texture, be open to microscopic changes and their meanings.

It is an approach that is reflected in the lexicon of seasonal words *(kigo)* used in Japanese poetry. By 1803, reports Haruo Shirane in his *Japan and the Culture of the Four Seasons* (2013), there were 2,600 approved seasonal topics, and 'seasons had become a fundamental means of categorizing the world'. This taxonomy works both ways. It demonstrates a deep understanding of and openness to continual change, but can also be restrictive, overly formalized and lacking in spontaneity – and there's the first of the elements of creative tension that underpin Japanese craft.

Seasonality emerged later in the trip when we were eating whisky *kaiseki* in Kyoto with chef Hashimoto and Shinji Fukuyo (see page 161). 'In certain cultures,' said the chef, 'they have spring lamb and autumn lamb, but here we have more.'

'That's because,' added Shinji, 'in the old way of calculating there are more than four seasons – there are 72.' He explains that in the old lunar calendar, the year was divided into 24 *sekki*, each of which was

Minkaen, the folk house museum in Kawasaki.

The smell of *hinoki* and firewood in an ancient house.

then subdivided into three *ko* of around five days each. Each had its own poetic name. We were talking in *Kusaretaru kusa hotaru to naru* (when fireflies rise from the rotten grass). Each has its own *hashiri, shun* and *nagori*. Being a geek about such things I went back to the hotel and downloaded an app telling me when each season started.

Becoming increasingly obsessed about this way of being attuned to change, I began to see it everywhere. Jota had already explained the 'seasons' of whisky maturation, but was it elsewhere? I wrote to Jota and Shinji wondering if you could apply *hashiri, shun* and *nagori* to tasting a whisky, as it too has a beginning, a peak in the middle of the mouth, and then a slow fade.

Shinji replied: '*Hashiri* is about expectation, a food that has not fully reached its prime – or a drink like Beaujolais Nouveau! Or a whisky that is very fresh and vivid, but not mature enough yet.

'*Shun* is the centre of the season and the best time to eat. As a whisky, this is a peak of maturation. *Nagori* is when people want to enjoy the final time, and at the same time anticipate the next season. We can also find some beauty in whisky that is overaged.

That is sometimes deep bitterness that reminds me of its beautiful maturation peak.

'We cannot enjoy the *hashiri* and *nagori* if we don't understand the quality of *shun*. When we enjoy both *hashiri* and *nagori* we also enjoy the *shun* in our imagination. The imagination can occasionally exceed the real sense.'

It was a lesson that made me start to taste in a different manner. It's an approach which shows how everything is impacting on you at this moment. The season forces you to be aware of freshness, but also of transience. I will never taste this glass in front of me again. The next time I pour this whisky I will have changed, as will the occasion, the temperature, the room. It will taste different if I'm drinking with friends or on my own.

You have to accept change.

Mars Shinshu

マルス信州蒸溜所

Tokyo to Mars

Time to leave Tokyo. A whisky-importer friend (of whom more later) had kindly not only lent us his Range Rover–now there's a strange sight on a Japanese highway–but one of his staff, who was also a friend, Ogachi-san, as driver and interpreter for our two-day trip to Mars, Hakushu and Chichibu. Having him drive allowed me to look out of the window and scribble, and Take to keep his trigger finger primed without the danger of crashing the car.

Mars Shinshu (to give it its full title) is a three-hour drive northwest towards the Southern Alps, through yet more tunnels which eventually release you into a mountain landscape, hills folded like crumpled green crêpe. It's a triangular landscape, with small villages, dotted with minuscule vegetable plots, huddling on the valley floor as if they are either respectful of the heights, or afraid of them. Maybe it's both. 'In the ancient period,' writes Haruo Shirane, 'untamed nature was often regarded as a bitter adversary, a land filled with wild and dangerous gods. In the mid- to late-Heain era [12th century CE] coppiced mixed forest appears as an intermediate zone of engagement.' The deep forests of *mizunara* and *chinquapin* were mostly left alone. The wild was kept at bay. This ambivalent relationship with nature would reappear throughout the trip.

We stop just before the southerly turnoff beside Lake Suwa. We're too late for the weird winter occurrence of a mountain ridge of ice that can form on its surface as the hot springs which are concentrated in the area percolate upwards, cracking the frozen surface and creating the *o-miwatari*, or passage of the gods. Deprived of this phenomenon, we browse among the shelves of the service station which, as is typical in Japan, contain not just the usual snacks and child-placating toys, but gift-wrapped regional specialities. This area is soba central and the store is filled with infinite variations of noodles. I swither about buying an armful, but then reckon there will be little chance of dried noodles surviving a three-week trip.

The importance of the regional speciality adds another layer to awareness of seasonality. A few years before on another trip to Mars Shinshu we'd stayed further north in the city of Matsumoto, mainly to drink in the great Pub Mahorobi. At some point, a chef had told us that there was a mountain nearby that was home to free-range pigs. 'We call them dancing pigs because when you eat the meat you too feel like dancing,' he claimed. He gave us an address to go and see them. Needless to say we failed.

Turning south, we ascend steadily towards Komaganc. As we are no longer at highway speed I open the window, listening to the birdsong as we pass alpine-style chalets and the slightly incongruous half-timbered Highland Hotel. The road is being twisted inexorably closer to the mountainside, bordered by pink, leggy pines, through which at one point wander a group of old-age pensioners with golf clubs. Maybe the local spot is a mix of pitch-and-putt and orienteering. Perhaps the clubs are to ward off dancing pigs.

A river–narrow, fast, creamy–veers close by. A crow sounds a warning and we're at the distillery, one which has confounded history and has risen, shaking off the mothballs and emerging into a new century.

The fast-running streams of the highlands flow beside the distillery.

MARS SHINSHU

That pig-hunting trip had taken place five years before, when a visit to the distillery had started as a one of those sad calls to a closed site (see These We Have Lost, page 106) but ended with the revelation that it was about to reopen. Since then things have moved on apace. It has been winning awards, there are new stills, and a new distiller – the quiet and thoughtful Koki Takehira.

The air is notably cooler. Mars sits at 800m (2,625ft), making it the highest distillery in Japan. The high valley through which we've driven is pressed between the lower slopes of Mount Komagatake to the west and Mount Tokura to the east.

The story of Mars is as appropriately odd as you might expect for a place with such an unusual name. Best to get that out of the way first. It was given its name after its parent company, Hombo, ran a competition. As it already had a *shōchū* brand called Star Treasury, some wiseacre suggested that the new plant be called Mars, or to be precise Shinshu Mars (sometimes just Shinshu). From 2017 it will be known as Mars Shinshu – and probably just Mars. I'm sticking to the last one.

Why, though, did a firm based in the southern city of Kagoshima pick this high, cool and remote location?

As ever it starts with water. That stream outside, like the water for the distillery, is flowing from the mountains: rock-polished, softened and abundant. Then there's the climate. 'The temperature differential is huge here,' explains Takehira; 'in summer it is 30° to 33°C (86° to 91°F). In winter it can be -10°C (14°F). Even in summer there is a huge difference between the day and night temperatures. That's going to affect not just the maturation cycle, but the way in which the alcohol vapour condenses – fast. The humidity also causes fogs, which are important for maturing whisky.' Outside sit the two original stills, tiny with oddly pointed lyne arms like elongated heron's bills, as if every effort was being made to squeeze the vapour into a tiny thread of flavour, adding focus.

It's easy to speak of Mars as being a lost distillery that has now been found, but it is more significant than that. It is a forgotten piece in the

The distillery has risen from the grave.

jigsaw of Japanese whisky history. Although only built in 1985, it has some-how always been there, a shadow in the background manifesting itself in different locations and dreams all the way back to the very start of the nation's whisky-making.

Whisky isn't just about the spirit running into the safe, or coming out of the cask. There are links all the way through, an interdependent net of occurrences. Flavours do not spring fully formed into life; they start as precursors, which can then bloom – or disappear – depending on the conditions.

Distilleries are the same, and the precursors of Mars were many. To understand them, you have to go back to a man called Kijiro Iwai. The approved story of the ancient period of Japanese whisky is that it was started by two men: Shinjiro Torii, the visionary, and Masataka Taket-suru, the distiller, who in 1920 was sent to Scotland to learn whisky-mak-ing. Who, though, sent Taketsuru? A firm called Settsu Shozu and, more specifically, his boss, Kijiro Iwai.

It was to Iwai that Taketsuru gave his report. Unfortunately, Settsu Shozu was by then in administration, and with no finance to start the project, Taketsuru left to work at Torii's new Yamazaki plant.

It wasn't until 1960 that Iwai's dream fully manifested itself. Hombo (run by his son-in-law) went into whisky-making in the wine-grow-

The new stills (below right) are larger than the originals (below) but are the same shape.

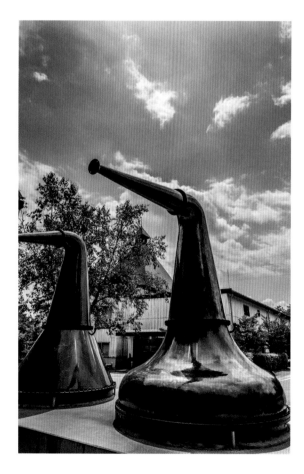

Steam is used to heat the stills.

ing region of Yamanashi. Using Taketsuru's notes and Iwai's expertise the whisky was in the big, smoky, old style. It was too old-fashioned for Japan, and nine years later it closed. The jinx had struck again.

In 1978 Hombo tried again, this time at its base in Kagoshima, where it made small amounts of whisky from minuscule new stills. Then, in 1985, Mars opened, using the original Yamanashi stills. Now the style was to change and become lighter, fruitier. The timing couldn't have been worse. The home market was about to turn away from whisky. In 1992, it closed.

Then, to most people's surprise, in 2011 it reopened. That's whisky for you. False starts, optimism, disappointment, trying again, never giving up. Mars is the little distillery which could.

Now, inside, all is new – as is the whisky-making approach. Takehira was originally a brewer and is using that background to create a new style (or styles) for Mars. 'We've changed the mashing regime, the fermentation – and the middle cut. In particular I'm paying attention to the wort.' Here is a major difference between Japanese and Scottish approaches to whisky.

Wort is the name for the sweet liquid that is drained off the mash tun. If the pumping is fast, some of the barley husk can be pulled through. This cloudy wort will in turn help to promote a cereal note in the final spirit. It's desirable in some distilleries, avoided in others. A gentle extraction gives clear wort and a fruitier result. In Scotland, 'clear' means there are no big bits. In Japan, however, 'clear' means just that. This is one reason for the whisky's 'transparency'. The lack of a heavy, dry, cereal

background (noticeable in most Scotches) helps to create part of Japanese whisky's 'transparent' nature.

'I've installed a wort clarity viewer,' he says, pointing to a sight glass on the pipe leading from the wash tun. 'We can check clarity just by holding our hands on the other side and noticing if we can see them. I'll look at pressure to ensure there's no compression in the mash tun, but it's really all done by hand.'

The two new stills are larger but with the same sharp-nosed shape as the originals. There's also a worm tub on the spirit still, which by reducing the amount of copper that comes in contact with the spirit vapour, adds a little extra weight to the final distillate.

'I've changed the cut points as well,' he says with a smile. 'It used to be a lot wider. We found complex aromas at the start of the run and wanted to retain them, but if the middle cut is long then we'll lose that intensity. So the best way to get the best heart was to make it shorter.'

The warehouse is steadily filling up with mainly ex-bourbon casks 'because they give a quicker maturation'. He looks around. 'During the silent period, there was no stock and no-one was trained in how to make whisky. When we reopened, we were starting from zero.'

Has that meant a change in style? 'It might be different, but we don't really have the full answer yet. So I am trying lots of things.' As well as ex-bourbon casks there are wine casks from Yamanashi, some *mizunara* – and *shōchū* casks as well.

'We're also looking at the effects of climate on the casks, so we have some casks ageing in Kagoshima, which is not only warmer, but only 60m (197 feet) above the sea. We've also put some into a warehouse in Yakushima island, which is even further south, hotter and more humid. All the heavy peaty stock is there. We're kind of making an island malt!'

We settle down for a tasting in the visitor centre. There are a lot of glasses: more than I expected. The experiments to find the soul of Mars have also involved using different yeasts. 'We're doing a four-day fermentation to get more fruity esters,' he explains. 'We have dried distiller's yeast, but also the old yeast type that was used here, and there's a beer yeast from Yamanashi and a different *Weissbier* yeast that I did a run of this year.' Stir in three different malt specifications – low, medium and heavy peated – and you can begin to see the possibilities.

'At the moment, we're making eight types, but we're still searching for the house style. We are looking at the possibilities of growing barley, and seeing whether we can plant *mizunara* in Nagano.'

It's a lot of extra work, though, I say, thinking of how unlikely all of this would be back home. He laughs. 'Why do things simply when you can make things interesting?'

Not only does the approach make perfect sense – the need to discover what an effectively new distillery is capable of – but it fits in with the Japanese approach of making multiple styles under one roof. The philosophy behind it also strikes me as being tied to the forensic approach that seems to exist within traditional crafts.

He nods. 'Japanese people like to find out smallest details. As a result of this inquiring mind we create something new. That is our craftsmanship.

Attention to detail 1: checking the level of a cask (top). Attention to detail 2: Takehira takes a sample (bottom).

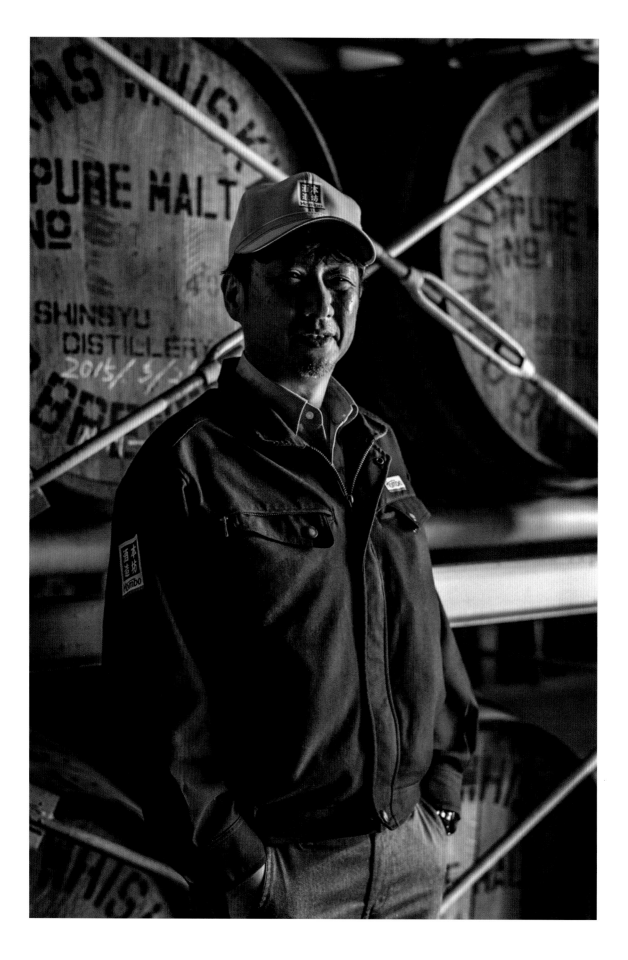

'One of our philosophies is to challenge ourselves and what we have been told. It's the only way to find our house style. In the future we might only make one style, but to find it we have to challenge the possibilities. That's also our craftsmanship – it's a quest.'

Does that mean a different approach to tradition? 'Changing is important, but sometimes not changing is as important, so we are always paying attention to what should remain and what should be improved. Those 19 years of silence made things difficult. The tradition wasn't passed on properly, so I've had to revive the method from the Iwai records. The mind of Iwai, his spirit, is still there. That is what we are now reviving.'

Takehira pauses. 'We will never close again. We will pass this on to the next generation.'

There is a determination in his words. Many of the newer international converts to Japanese whisky will have no idea of how precarious the situation was for close on 25 years. They have only known it in the good times, when Japanese whisky began to appear in export markets. There is little sense of a back story – and why should there be one?

The shorthand is that Japanese whisky has been made since 1923 and has been made in the same way, slowly gaining in importance ever since. Well, it has not been made in the same way, and neither has it all been plain sailing. Any distiller will tell you that whisky is cyclical; it is buffeted by the winds of change, caught on the tides of fashion. Distillers have to second-guess what will be sold many years in the future and anticipate what styles, what flavours, will be popular.

Mars was one of many distilleries that were caught in that perfect storm of the late 1980s when a generation turned away from whisky and those who remained shifted their love towards Scotch. That it has now risen is testament to a resilient belief in quality and also a greater understanding of the vagaries of the market. The one theme that runs through the story of Mars is that of hope. They will succeed, because that is the spark which has always driven them on.

There is inevitably only a limited amount of bottling from Mars as stock needs to be built up – and a 25-year hole in inventory has to be bridged. One way came with the elegant **Maltage 3+25**, a vatting of three-year-old malts from Hombo's Yamanashi and Kagoshima distilleries that had been aged for 25 years at Mars. The few remaining Mars-distilled casks have also appeared as single casks or been used in a selection of blends such as Twin Alps and Iwai Tradition, which also contain some imported spirit. Both are sweet, fruity drams suitable for mixing.

The focus, however, has to be on the future. A selection of low-peat whisky aged for four years in ex-bourbon casks, but made from different yeasts, gives an insight into current thinking – and the often dramatic differences that can result.

Dry yeast gives a lightly floral nose with some lemon, a little bamboo, and a hint of turmeric. The sweet and slightly thick distillery style comes through on the palate with added custard and banana. The use of an ale yeast adds more weight, with richer orchard fruits, orange rather than lemon. Sweet again, this is softer and more rounded.

Using the distillery's old yeast strain changes things further, bringing out a phenolic edge, some pear and a more vegetal attack. While the fruits are there, it remains slightly more dumb on the tongue, although there is a gingery kiss on the end.

A five-year-old cask sample of the heavy-peated variant aged in a sherry hogshead is clear and ripe with added smoked meat on the nose. The palate shows sweetness with the sherry adding a nutty depth. Precise, focused and hugely promising.

Currently the only 100 per cent Mars-distilled bottled product is **Komagatake 3-year-old** (57% ABV), which has been aged in ex-sherry and bourbon casks before a year in ex-wine casks. It's the latter that have the upper hand. Sunset-gold in colour, it shows surprising breadth for a whisky of its age, quite fleshy, with cooked plum, cherry jam, rose and a hint of smoke. The distillery's thick, sweet character is there alongside rosehip syrup and caramelized fruit. Precocious.

Though limited in volume, the whiskies from Mars are winning plaudits.

Mars to Hakushu

It's time to depart. The birds are singing. It's a place that has been saved, and is not just saved and returning to those founding principles but moving forward as well. You might expect Japanese distillers to be worried. The stocks are an issue, and there's a possibility that, when they return to balance, the world's attention might have gone somewhere else. Yet here, and at Gotemba the day before, there is real belief that this is the time for innovation, new ideas and rebirth. With these thoughts, we climb back into the car and head to Hakushu. We turn the corner and the woods envelop us once more. Mars, somehow, disappears into the trees. There is often something modest about distilleries; they hide in woods, around corners. They give up their secrets seemingly reluctantly. They are also very much part of a landscape, not the industrial plants that many imagine, but sited because of water, and climate – manifestations of place.

Heading into the woods.

Hakushu

白州蒸溜所

Mars to Hakushu

Hakushu is only 50km (31 miles) due east of Mars, but the not-inconsiderable lump of the Minami Alps in between means that we have to take the long way round. We grab fuel, water, sandwiches, *onigiri* rice balls and unhealthy snacks at the nearest petrol station, then it's back to Lake Suwa once again and southeast on the Chuo Expressway before nicking off at Kobuchisawa and twisting down the hill to the distillery.

Hakushu is another distillery that does a good job of hiding itself: no inconsiderable feat given that for a time it was the largest single malt distillery in the world, but the approach has changed dramatically since those days.

Hakushu suffers, if that's the right term, from second-child syndrome. Yamazaki, close to Kyoto and Osaka, is the foundation stone of Japanese whisky, Suntory's flagship malt. Hakushu has long just got on quietly with producing for the firm's blends. Even when it belatedly emerged as a single malt it did so *sotto voce*. Maybe that's appropriate, though.

Like Mars, it is a distillery that you seem to chance upon, which is surprising, given its size. You wind down the hill towards it, heading inexorably into heavily forested mountain slopes. The serrated lines of granite peaks scrape against the sky. Surely there cannot be anything here? Then, suddenly, you are next to a saluting gatekeeper at the barrier.

Though the distillery's footprint is enormous, the buildings are hidden within that deep forest. This site is as much national park as it is industrial site. Even the word *Hakushu* sounds like the breeze through the pines. It's a whisky that whispers with the evanescent scents of the wood: fern and moss, wild herbs, pine needles, and a drift of woodsmoke. It's complex, layered, subtle, and as discreet as a spritz of perfume on the hem of a kimono in summer. That's not to say it is wimpy. Hakushu has a quiet presence.

Hakushu sits within a forest.

HAKUSHU

I'm met by an old friend, Mike Miyamoto, former manager here and at Yamazaki, ex-global brand ambassador and for a time Suntory's representative in Glasgow – his daughter still has a broad Glaswegian accent. Alongside is Ono-san, who rejoices in the grand title of Hakushu's executive general manager. Like Mike he's a long server, joining Suntory in 1989. His title gives you an idea perhaps of the scale of this operation.

It's easy to be seduced by the figures reeled out about Hakushu: the 97 hectares (204 acres) covered by the site, its 700m (2,297ft) altitude, the 200,000 visitors it gets a year, the 600,000 casks in its warehouses, the 30m litres (6.6m gallons) a year it was producing at its peak.

Numbers cannot reveal a whisky's soul. To rely on them as auguries of quality is to miss what lies beneath. Hakushu wasn't built here because there was space to suit Suntory's grand vision; the site was chosen in 1973 because of climate, water, geology. Nature dictates Hakushu as much as science and economics.

It might not be as big as it was in the 1980s, when it was the largest malt distillery in the world and the original distillery (Hakushu West) was joined by a companion facility (Hakushu East), but it is still substantial. And here's the thing: it manages to combine the ultra-modern – at times it seems a malt distillery of a possible future – while at the same time retrofitting traditional approaches to whisky-making. That, it strikes me, is a very Japanese approach. Too many distilleries around the world fall back on the glibly empty phrase of being 'a fusion between the past and the future'. It usually means that while the stills haven't changed shape, the manager now has an espresso machine in her office.

Equally, when modern techniques or equipment are introduced it is a sign of the distillery continuing to use technology to move further away from the confusion of the past. The reason given is 'efficiency' – using technology to ensure that a spirit character is maintained more effectively. It's an approach that has some merit.

At Hakushu, however, Suntory has managed to apply its deep understanding of whisky-making from a scientific perspective while reverting to techniques which, in Scotland at least, have been long-regarded as archaic and 'inefficient'. This willingness to reintroduce 'lost' practices is something that Japanese whisky has always done. Its distillers have never been scared to change, sometimes radically. The market has moved on? We can change. New learning offers us greater insights? We can change. Tradition, in other words, is flexible and fluid—respected but not formalized.

Mars this morning might have been an extreme example of how timing can go badly wrong, but that ethos of 'we can only survive by looking hard at what we do and finding the new path' is alive there. It is simply writ larger here. That original stillhouse fell silent in 2000 and now production is focused on Hakushu East.

It was built as a response to the increased demand for blended whisky during the boom time. As a result, it has long been making multiple distillates. Today, there are even more. Four types of malt—unpeated, low-, medium-, and heavily peated—are utilized.

We're at the mash tun, which holds 16 tonnes (the temptation to break into Tennessee Ernie Ford's hit is almost overwhelming). Again, like at Mars, clear wort is the aim. 'Cloudy wort covers the aroma like clouds over the sun,' says Mike. 'We ran a lot of experiments with clear and cloudy worts and discovered clear gives a "clear" aroma. We really respect tradition, but there are many areas where we can innovate, and mashing is part of that.'

New stills were installed in 1910.

I've already seen the effect of clear wort in the delicacy of Gotemba and the sweetness of Mars, but that limpid transparency comes into greater focus here at Hakushu. This, particularly the peated variants, is a challenging whisky to make. Smoke can be a dominant force, elbowing the more subtle aromas out of the way, adding a potentially unbalancing dryness. Here though, even the smokiest new-make has a clarity to it, allowing all of the aromas to have equal status. They have elegance and some persistence, rather than weight.

'It takes time to get the filter bed to settle in the mash tun,' explains Ono. 'We must allow that time so that we are getting no compression of the bed. It then will help us get that estery quality and some richness in aroma.'

Different yeasts are also used in the three-day ferment. 'Distiller's yeast and ale yeast are pitched at the same time,' says Ono. 'The distiller's will help give a consistent yield [the measurement of litres of alcohol for each tonne of malt]. The brewer's yeast doesn't help with yield, but does build that extra layer of complexity.'

So is this one of the things that makes Japanese whisky Japanese? 'We believe that the traditional way of making whisky has a lot to do with character,' says Mike. 'The fact that Scotland has moved away from that might make us "Japanesey" because we are following an old Scottish style! Scientifically, we don't know why brewer's yeast works, but through sensory tests we'd argue that it gives complexity and body to the spirit.'

Wooden washbacks are used to help create specific characters.

Hakushu's column still is used for experimental grain whiskies.

The fact that fermentation takes place in wooden washbacks (18 in total) is another element in the Hakushu jigsaw. Most whisky-lovers treat the tun room as being the support band which you half listen to in preparation for the main double bill of stills and wood.

Distillation, however, is only about concentrating and selecting existing flavours, most of which are created in fermentation. In whisky, all the sugar is converted into alcohol within 48 hours. Extending the time in the fermenter won't make the wash any stronger, but it will help to trigger lactobacilli. To help produce a wider range of styles the fermentation times at Hakushu will also vary.

The lactobacilli begin to act on the wash after the yeast has died. Some dine on the dead yeast cells; others attack sugars which the yeast cannot convert; others only come to life after 70 hours when the acidity is higher. In other words, they help to generate flavour: in Hakushu's case, fragrant esters, and add a creaminess to the spirit. Another layer of complexity.

This, though, is a modern distillery, one where stainless-steel washbacks might seem more appropriate. 'But if it's steel with a smooth surface there is nowhere for those lactobacilli to hide,' explains Miyamoto. 'Wood is porous and offers crevices where they can survive.'

To add another element to the story, it has been discovered that each distillery has its own unique colony of lactobacilli which, in turn, could be one reason why you can only make Hakushu at Hakushu.

Another reason lies in the almost ridiculous collection of stills. You don't quite know where to start. While most distilleries have one shape for the wash and one for the spirit, here all of that convention has been

hurled over the mountain. There are eight pairs of stills made in seven different types: fat or tall, thin or plump. Lyne arms go up, down – some can be detached and switched to another angle; some go into condensers, others go into worms. Run in pairs, every one will produce a different spin on the Hakushu style. At this point, your head begins to hurt with the possibilities.

Their burnished surfaces emit an almost eerie glow made stranger by the weird dim green light, giving the whole space the air of some dragon's cave. Voices automatically drop in volume, becoming so soft that sibilants get lost in the sound of the roar from the wash stills – which are all direct-fired rather than steam-heated, another almost obsolete technique that has been reintroduced here.

'In the past, we had direct fire on both sides,' says Mike, 'but we did a lot of experimentation and have switched all the spirit stills to steam coil. We've kept direct fire on the wash side, because the first distillation has to do with building in character. In the second, fire has little effect because that is about refining and selecting only.'

Throughout its history, Hakushu has expanded and contracted and the distillery has now expanded once again. We stand beside the new pair of stills that were added in the most recent expansion in 2010 – further evidence of the new long-term confidence in Japanese whisky. 'We've actually imitated the Yamazaki pots,' says Ono, 'but without the bulge. It's to allow us to get a more rich and robust complexity. We're not making Yamazaki, though!'

Hakushu West had massive stills, making light spirit.

The Matrix-like warehouse, in which many different styles and cask types are aged.

Capacity may have risen, but Mike adds, 'It is not just about making more, which might appear to be the case. This is also about making more different styles as well.'

How important, then, is tradition? "We believe that tradition and innovation must be combined. It's a difficult balance to achieve. When, for example, we need to replace or add more stills we might not stick to the old shape – that's not tradition in a Scottish whisky-making sense. It is working with tradition in a fluid way.

'At Yamazaki [in the 1920s and 1930s], there was uncertainty. We were seeking in the darkness, so to speak. Hakushu was designed from the beginning. We knew what whiskies we'd like to make here, but didn't know what character it could make.' To an extent, therefore, the changes that have taken place have been dictated by the distillery itself.

Those changes are not finished. As well as the new pot stills, a company-designed small double column still (an 18-plate analyser and 40-plate rectifier) was installed in 2010. 'We needed variety even in grain whisky,' explains Ono. 'This is so small that we can run smaller batches and use various different kinds of grains. We have malt so we can run 100 per cent malt through it, or rye, wheat, or corn. As we can also take the spirit off at any plate in the rectifier; we can collect different flavours. We love to do something different!'

And is that what helps to make it Japanese? 'The aim has been to produce a flavour that suits the gentle Japanese palate,' says Ono, 'but also I think the Japanese approach has always been to try and pursue perfection. It's in the blood.'

Staves ready for coopering into casks.

'And that is part of the tradition,' chips in Mike. 'Improve the character and quality, never be complacent, never be satisfied … that's the attitude.'

I was beginning to wonder if this could be squared with my attempt to align whisky-making with traditional craft practices. Japan's traditions, we are always told, are established on a reverence for the past, and are fixed in time and method. On the other hand, modern Japan is apparently all about copying, adapting and conceivably improving. Are they two different approaches?

We head into the forest that surrounds the distillery. Above rise the slopes of Mount Kaikomagatake, its granite slowly worn away by the rains and snowmelt, the streams joining the Ojira River at an alluvial fan of white sand—the meaning of the word 'Hakushu'.

Warehouses emerge, laced by ivy, hidden in the trees like some lost city. With every year that passes you feel they are being drawn into the landscape. The ivy cladding, it transpires, is deliberate and acts as a covering which prevents heat loss, the same reason that half of each warehouse is buried underground to keep an equable temperature. This is still a high alpine setting with wide temperature fluctuations: 5°C (41°F) in winter and 25°C (77°F) in summer. 'It is considerably cooler and less humid here in the Alps than at Yamazaki,' says Mike, 'and maturation takes longer.'

Maybe it also helps to retain that cool herbal freshness which typifies Hakushu, as if the tendrils of the forest have slowly inveigled their way into the whisky's aroma. Inside, caged in metal racks, it's like a scene from *The Matrix*. While most of the new-make is aged in American oak barrels and hogsheads, Hakushu is also aged in new American oak puncheons and European oak sherry (both of these are matured at Suntory's Ohmi facility). I try to do the maths. Four types of malt, eight pairs of stills which could give 32 different options. Stir in five different types of cask and … my brain begins to hurt.

Close by – but strictly off the tourist trail – is Suntory's cooperage, a huge hanger of sweet-smelling oak, the dry, chocolate scent of char, and quiet industry. Tools, dull metal and hand-worn handles. All around are horizontal forests of bundled staves, each one of which is checked, cleaned up, and then re-assembled into either barrels or hogsheads. If distillers work by smell, coopers work by sound: the creak of windlass on wood, the ring of hammer on metal hoops, a rasp as the croze is cut, a strange mix of the violent and the gentle, angles and pressure.

Before we leave the distillery, we take a quick walk through the old stillhouse. The last time I was there it was a forgotten hulk, the 12 massive stills looming through the dim light. Stand in their presence and the final words of Shelley's poem *Ozymandias* might echo through the gloom: 'Look on my works, ye mighty, and despair'. Their size is a testament to the volumes deemed necessary to fuel the Japanese whisky boom; their silence, a dumb testament to its precipitate decline. In their place, a newer, smaller-scale, more highly flexible alternative.

'Two years after the building of the second still house [1983] was the peak of the category in Japan,' says Mike. 'It was huge – Suntory Old was selling 12 million cases a year in Japan alone. We didn't need styles; we needed one style and that's what this distillery provided: a light single malt as a filler for our blends. Then whisky began to decline, and as it did so

The forest setting seems to be reflected in Hakushu's whiskies.

the purpose of distilling became different. Now we need smaller volumes, but greater variety. That's why this still house is no longer needed.'

In simple terms, the switch took place from blend to malt – but it was by no means a seamless transition. 'When we built the new still house we didn't even think of single malt,' he adds. 'Though Yamazaki was launched as a brand in 1984, we weren't sure of what would happen in time. Remember that even when we shifted focus from blend to malt in the 1990s, as an industry we were all struggling.'

What was a darkened mausoleum, a lesson about the vagaries of a market and over-reaching, is now a chandeliered monument to the fact that change is needed. Receptions are held in the space, the stills now seemingly benign presences as the backdrop. That was then; we've moved on.

What, then, is the Suntory style? 'A never-give-up spirit,' responds Mike immediately. 'Even during that 25 years of decline we believed in our whisky. Torii's motto can be translated as "go for it" and that's the attitude. I've been with the firm for 37 years and we have always been experimenting, always going for it. Though it might not always work, you have to try it. That's the founder's spirit.'

Perhaps I've been looking at this in an either/or fashion, that something can either be ultra-traditional or modern. Instead, the tradition is alive and fluid. There is a tendency to think of whisky in terms of a rigid continuity – a distillery style is fixed and improved upon, but remains constant. It is there like a fingerprint, a double helix of spirit and cask. The reality is more nuanced. Change is not just accepted, but welcomed. This is how things are: seasons, people, knowledge, understanding. To stand still is to reject natural process; it ends in you being left, fossilized, entombed in rock. Rather, and appropriately enough in this setting, you have to move with the wind in the pines.

The ivy-clad warehouses seem to sink into the landscape (top). Mike Miyamoto reflects on a job well done (bottom).

白州蒸溜所

Hakushu is set up to produce as wide a range of variants on a style as possible, and a tasting of some new-makes and blending components can easily baffle you with the knowledge that there are so many other possibilities from which to draw.

The unpeated new-make is a good marker, already showing the distillery's light, green, grassy character alongside sweet melon fruits and an umami-like texture. Medium-peated is equally fresh but slightly drier, thanks to the smoke, while the heavy-peated variant takes you into a forest bonfire although the spirit itself remains precise and quite delicate. Now, stir in all of the options in terms of stills … well … you get my drift.

The new-make from the grain stills is equally fascinating. The corn-based has good weight – it is more powerful than Chita's (see page 114) heaviest with added red fruits. A mashbill containing 40 per cent rye has rose-scented talcum powder, allspice and raspberry. A wheat-based distillate has tighter focus and intensity with some sweetness, and a more overt acidity.

Of the bottled selection, the new(ish) **Distiller's Reserve** (43% ABV) shows what should be done with No Age Statement whiskies. It has sweet melon, some basil but a soft sweet fruitiness that hints at apricot. The palate is well-rounded with cool cucumber but a real mid-palate presence. The **12-year-old** (43% ABV) by contrast seems lighter, with fresh herbs, mint, fir trees and a tiny hint of smoke that works neatly with the acidity on the finish. It is perhaps the quintessential example of Hakushu's understated calm.

As is common with Suntory's approach, the **18-year-old** (43% ABV) marks a step-change into richer territory, though this being Hakushu there is still a restraining hand at work. Think more ginger and chocolate, plum and almond. The palate shows a touch of tropical fruit and sweet melon. The smoke is also more apparent. At the more esoteric end is the **25-year-old** (43% ABV), which shows a deep waxy maturity with baked/dried sweet fruits but still a mossy underpinning. The tannins are soft (say, compared to Yamazaki) and that acidity is still there.

The woodland malt (below).
Hakushu Highball (below right).

Whisky-*dō*

We head off into the dark, up an increasingly narrow road to one of the alpine-style inns that dot the region. The reception area is deserted. Mike takes us back outside to a cabin which is both kitchen and dining room. We sit around a firepit. Highballs arrive immediately. Strong ones. Proper ones. Hakushu ones. 'To freshen us up.' The smoke of the fire mingles with the delicate smokiness of the drink. We are regularly refreshed as we swap stories and jokes.

A long, gently paced meal starts. Everything is local: foraged, grown, killed, or caught within a 10km (*c.*6 mile) radius around the restaurant. It's vaguely Italian-esque, but with a Japanese twist. Trout and venison, fresh veg and wasabi, three-year-old miso, hop buds, smoked duck, homemade tofu and a plate of vegetables with a miso-based *bagna cauda*. The same themes of the afternoon emerge again: the taking, the inspiration, the absorbing, and the evolution into something that speaks of place. The approach at this auberge is no different to that in the distillery or the cooperage.

'Of course it becomes Japanese,' says Mike as another round of Highballs arrives. 'We are Japanese and we are in Japan! Its flavours are around us and we approach everything in a Japanese fashion. Everything we make is "something-*dō*". It means "the way" and can be applied to tea, flowers, food … and whisky.

'As Suntory we never see whisky-making as "production". We try and pursue quality and character. That is whisky-*dō* and whisky-making is the art of craft and nature.' He gives a quiet smile. 'People say that's crazy, that "it's only whisky", but we take it deeper – it's *the way* of whisky, and the art of whisky.'

Of course. That's it. That's what sets it apart. It is simply the way in which things are done in Japan. It is inevitable that something which involves a creative process will be influenced by this attitude – an approach that is the tradition of craftsmanship.

We leave to sit outside with a Hakushu 18-year-old around another fire, watching the wood glow and slumping into ash, whisky on the lips, conversation ebbing and flowing around our circle, shapes forming in the embers.

Dōgen's (1200–53, founder of the Sōtō school of Zen) metaphor for existence and time comes into focus. 'Firewood becomes ash. Ash cannot become firewood again. However, we should not view ash as after and firewood as before. We should know that firewood … dwells in firewood and has its own before and after … ash stays in the position of ash with its own before and after. Life is a position in time, death is a position in time. This is like winter and spring …' Each to be noticed, appreciated and allowed to pass. Seasons, sips, moments in time.

We drive home in thick fog, inching down the mountain from the campfires. I'm left at the Hotel Key Forest. It turns out I'm the only guest.

The room is magnificent and minimalist. Smell of woodsmoke in my hair, I take out some Gary Snyder. It may seem strange to quote American poets in a book on Japanese whisky, but he taught me about Japan, planted the seed, and his writing continues to nurture it. I'll always have one or other of his books on my travels. This time I'd grabbed his volume of essays, *The Practice of the Wild*. For some reason I turned to one, *Off the Path, Off the Trail*, which I had read many times. On one level it's an essay about the wild and Dōgen's maxim that 'practice is the path', which is maybe why it sprang to mind.

Its words suddenly took on a different meaning. In it, Snyder writes, 'Another reading of *dao* [*Ch'i*: way, road, trail] is the practice of an active craft. In Japan, *dao* is pronounced *dō* … "

He goes on to recount the stages of a craftsman's life, starting with the rigours of apprenticeship, often under the tutelage of a cranky master. 'For an apprentice, there was just this one study. Then the apprentice was gradually inducted into some not so obvious moves, standards of craft, and in-house working secrets. The apprentice also began to experience what it was to be "one with your work."'

Maybe I'm on the way.

Chichibu

秩父蒸溜所

Hakushu to Chichibu

Woken at 4am by the dawn chorus: cuckoos doing their rounds, a woodpecker drumming on some dead tree, unidentified others buzzing and singing. Serves me right for keeping the balcony door open. I wander around the silent hotel. On each floor there's a vitrine with sculptures (*dogū*) from the later stages of Japan's neolithic Jomon period which ran from 14,000 to 300BCE. Odd figures with wedge heads and slanted eyes, or goggle-eyed aliens, all with complex whorls of decoration.

This was also the period when pottery vessels began to be used for cooking – and which saw the start of fermentation. Here are the precursors of *koji*, miso, *nattō*, soy, *tsukemono* (pickled vegetables), sake, mirin, beer, wine … and whisky. This is a bubbly, yeasty country.

For some bizarre reason, next door to the hotel there is a museum dedicated to the New York artist Keith Haring, which I race around, thinking about the strange links between some of his patterns and the *dogū*. Nothing's new. It just changes.

Ogachi and Take are waiting for me as I return, drenched again. It's an interminable drive to Chichibu.

The most direct route is a little more than 130km (80 miles), but as it goes through the mountains and it's raining the decision is made to take the highway.

The dreary weather kills conversation. Take puts his camera away and dozes. Even he would find it hard to take anything of interest when we seem to be driving through a permanent car wash. It's hard to raise the spirits on days like this, when there are no mountains to see and the only aim is simply getting to the destination. I'm also feeling guilty that I was the only one staying in the swanky hotel. Not even the thought that rain is just whisky waiting to be born does anything to alleviate the mood.

The road swings so far to the southeast that we begin to flirt with Tokyo's gravitational pull – at one point I think that Ogachi, seeing signs for Shinjuku, has just decided to take us back.

As we hook north, then west, the rain starts to ease and, finally, there is the turning for Chichibu. The clouds are like steam rising off the mountains. Take has his camera out again.

A mysterious path into the forest above Chichibu.

CHICHIBU

秩父蒸溜所

Each time I go to Chichibu there's something new. This small distillery, two valleys to the northwest of the town, has become a university of whisky, and a beacon for new distillers around the world. Of course owner Ichiro Akuto is too modest to accept any such notions. He, in turn, praises what the big boys are doing, pointing out, not unreasonably, that they have the money, volume and clout to make bigger waves than he.

Still, the fact that he is in contact with his counterparts at the majors is a significant step. A decade ago, none of the firms would even talk to each other. Now there is an almost collegiate atmosphere, on the production side at least.

He's there to meet us, along with his global brand ambassador, Yumi Yoshikawa. I first met him in Scotland when he kept popping up at cooperages, coppersmiths and tastings, sourcing what he needed for his dream.

I came here not long after the distillery opened in 2008, and have returned regularly to catch up. Each time there have been new additions, new developments and a widening of Ichiro's holistic vision of creating a distillery that speaks of its place.

For example, they're now malting, one tonne at a time, and the barley is local. In fact, they've grown some of it themselves. Of course they have; it's what they do. Any time there is a new part of the process being researched, the team goes to the source – to the masters – and takes a crash course on how it is done. They wanted to malt some of their own requirements? They all went to Crisp Maltings in Norfolk to learn. They wanted to grow barley? They sat on tractors and planted it, then harvested it.

Five tonnes are being malted this year (the aim is for the local barley to make up 10 per cent of the distillery's requirements) and by sheer good fortune, the first batch is being distilled that day. In Ichiro's vision, it's a logical step, helping further to bind the distillery to the community. There was no heritage of barley cultivation here – this is soba country – but the fields will lie empty after that has been harvested. 'After we started to talk of how we make make malt in the UK,' he explains, 'local farmers who

The pagoda of Chichibu's kiln helps to process local barley.

wanted to utilize their land in winter asked if we might be interested if they grew barley. It's fun—and they earn money.'

Different varieties are being trialled. 'Sainohosi is harvested pre-rainy season, then there's a two-row mountain variety, Myosi-Nijo. We're also trialling old varieties like the low-yielding Golden Melon, which was the first barley used for whisky-making in Japan. It grows at a higher altitude, is low-yielding, but is harvested late—in the rainy season.'

'Low yield' means he gets less alcohol per tonne; something which would drive accountants bonkers. It might, Ichiro would counter, have a different flavour; it might just open up new possibilities.

It's a significant move, because for decades all of the malt used by Japanese distillers has been imported—from the UK, Europe, Australia. This is a rice-growing culture and as the industry expanded, the land couldn't support the volumes needed—and it was expensive.

Maybe the decision also comes from Ichiro's need to reinforce his own roots. His ancestors started brewing sake in Chichibu in 1625. When the firm's distillery in Hanyu closed (see page 107) he decided to start again. 'If I'd had lots of money I'd have searched all over Japan, but fortunately I had experienced sake-brewing here, and I knew the water was good for brewing. It's also hard to find good land to set up a new distillery, so I decided to start here, where I was born.'

From the outset, Chichibu has also used peated malt for one of its expressions. All of this has come from Crisp, but now some local peat is being trialed and, yes, the team has learned how to dig it and studied how kilning works. It smells of incense, apparently.

Chichibu's washbacks are made from *mizunara*.

We take off our shoes, pop on rubber slippers and enter the one-room operation. Everything is going on simultaneously: the mill is running, the mash tun is being filled, the stills are on, casks are being prepared, bottles are being filled and labelled. All is movement.

By the mill, an old-style 'shoogle box' is being employed by one of the team to double-check the grind. Three horizontal layers are separated by different sizes of mesh. Pop the ground barley (grist) in the top, put on the lid on and shake ('shoogle' in Scots) vigorously. Then weigh the three parts to check your ratio. 'He needs to work harder,' jokes Ichiro. I find a samba by Jorge Ben on my iPhone. If the sweat pouring from the kid is anything to go by, it seems to have the right rhythm.

At the mash tun, a new graduate is being taught by a young guy who also looks as if he's just left school. They watch every plash of the water and grist as if one imperfectly formed droplet could maybe compromise the quality.

The tank itself is tiny, holding only one tonne of grist. The mash is allowed to settle for 30 minutes, during which starch is converted. 'It might be stirred gently but only before it is drained. We want clear wort.'

We clamber up ladders to look into the washbacks, which are made from very expensive *mizunara* (see page 90). Just for aesthetics? 'I had actually thought about stainless steel, but I have a friend who works with wood and he proposed this. I was really happy. He reckons that there might be a different type of lactobacillus [which Mike Miyamoto has described; see page 59] living in *mizunara*, so there's a possibility of different types of flavour being made.

'You can tell the lactobacillus activity by measuring the acidity, so we don't think in terms of time, but pH. We're needing to get it down to four. If it's at that point, we get the esters and complexity we want. So we'll vary the length of the ferment depending on what happens. If it's above that, then we'll keep it in there.' He absent-mindedly smooths the side of one of them. 'Every one of these is different, but if you want an average it's 90 hours.'

It's here that you begin to understand the mix of intuition, experience, creativity and growing confidence that is at work in Chichibu. This is not and never has been Hanyu Mark 2. 'In any case, Chichibu's environment affects the character.'

Spirit is running through the two small (2,000-litre/440-gallon) stills. Unlike in Scotland, where spirit safes are locked and distillers have to rely on experience and instruments to make the cut, here there's a glass sitting, ready for use.

'We always cut by flavour,' says Ichiro, 'and so the actual cut point might change. We'll usually start collecting at around 72 or 73% ABV then come off at 63% for the unpeated and 61% for the peated. In winter, though, as the water temperature into the condenser is low we'll get a heavier spirit. Winter-distilled spirit is better for long-term maturation.' Here come those seasons again.

Constant checking: receiver tank (below) and spirit safe (below right).

This is to do with copper conversation. The longer the spirit vapour is in contact with copper the lighter it will be. Because the water coming into the condenser is colder in winter, the surface temperature is lower, so the conversion back to liquid is quicker and the spirit is heavier.

All of this is testing what the distillery can do. As Mike Miyamoto had alluded at Hakushu, these are living entities. I look around. The whole place is pulsing with energy, the sweet smell of the mash, the head-jolting prickle from the washbacks, the swirling complexities rising from the spirit safe, and in time this will be joined by the thick fungal scent of the warehouse. A living process.

If Chichibu is to work, if it is to survive, Ichiro has to explore all the possibilities even if his modesty means he continually downplays the significance of what he is doing. 'We're just small,' he says regularly. 'We're still learning.' He's right. The production levels here are minuscule compared to the majors and things are still so new, so experimental, that he's right to suggest that Chichibu is still at a malleable stage. The team is learning, the distillery is finding its feet. The two sides need to work together.

Writers and whisky geeks (and writers who are whisky geeks) want it all now. We are all excited by the possibilities unfolding here. 'Calm down,' Ichiro says. 'Whisky takes time. We will get there.' You can understand the impatience, though. Chichibu was the start of a new whisky era in Japan – and it was available (albeit in tiny quantities) internationally. At that time there was only Suntory and Nikka. Gotemba was domestic, Karuizawa (see page 106) was closed, Mars forgotten.

Held tight – a band around the *mizunara* washback (above). Ichiro Akuto, holistic visionary (opposite).

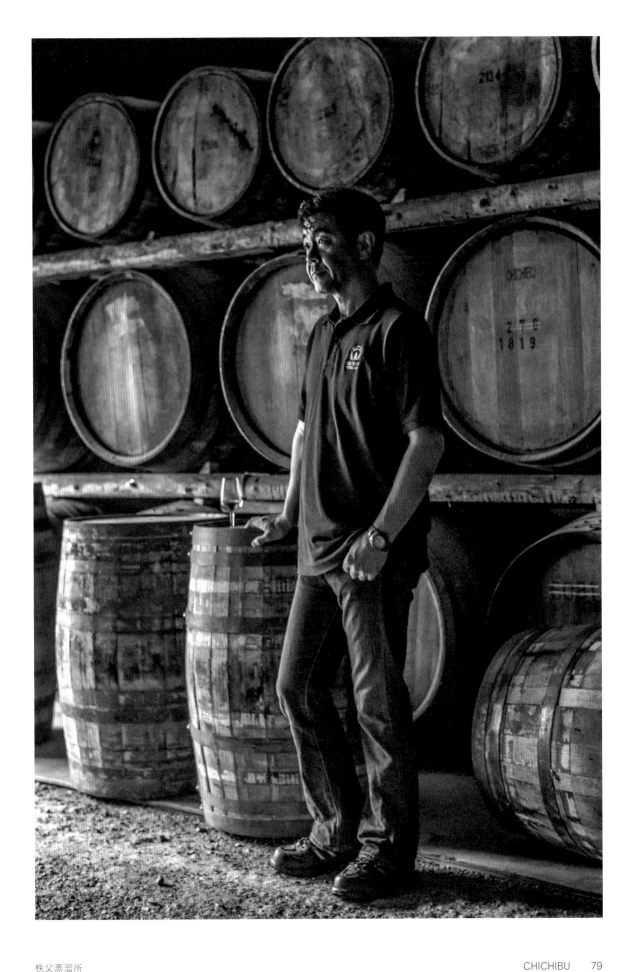

At times you wondered whether there might be something of the emperor's new clothes about the accolades Chichibu received from its first release – as happened with Karuizawa where people's critical faculties were put on hold because it was, by then, rare. But Chichibu was great from the word go. The concern wasn't its quality, but who else would follow Ichiro's example. He couldn't carry the hopes of a newly diverse industry on his shoulders.

It's a place of surprises. I glance at Take. Like me, he's got a huge grin on his face, albeit a bemused one. He'd seen it as well. It was hard not to. Not many distilleries have a giant wooden egg in the middle of the floor. It could be an art installation. Perhaps a giant wooden chicken was going to be lowered on top.

'Ichiro? The egg?'

'Ah!' he says, laughing, as if it was a surprise to him as well. It turns out it's from top French cooperage Taransaud and has been made for the wine industry. The shape, the firm claims, creates a gentle vortex allowing the wine to pick up greater mouthfeel. 'They asked if we wanted to see what would happen if we used it for marrying mature whiskies. So here it is! It holds ten casks, so we are using it as a kind of solera vat' (never fully emptying it, in other words, so as to get consistency and some depth from older whiskies).

And? 'It does seem to be getting more mellow.'

Filling casks at Chichibu.

Chichibu has become a university of whisky.

There is this element of 'what if?' about Chichibu. The rapidly filling warehouses (the fourth has just been built and will be filled in a year's time) are packed with every type of cask imaginable: barrels, hogsheads and puncheons from American oak, European oak ex-sherry butts and hogsheads; French oak ex-white and red wine, port and Madeira, new *mizunara*, rum, grappa, Cognac – and tequila. Brand-new casks and refills and Ichiro's own invention, the tiny *chibidaru* ('cute casks', literally) with heads of either white oak or *mizunara*. Some will be for full-term maturation, other for finishing; some might be for both.

'We are a very new distillery. In Scotland, distilleries stick to ex-sherry or ex-bourbon because they have a long history and they have found the right casks, but we are new so I like to try as many as possible to find the best casks for this distillery.'

'And?' I blurt out (there's that writerly impatience again).

'It's still too early to say what will be the best. It's very difficult.'

The final new development lies down the hill in the shed next to where the last remnants of Karuizawa sit. It's a purpose-built cooperage. 'We were always going to visit [cooper] Mizuo Saito in Saitama for his experience. Eventually we decided we should ask him to teach us how to make casks. Just so we would know, not that we ever wanted to do it.

'In 2012, he decided to close because he was old and had no successor.' Ichiro looks around the unit. 'All of this old machinery would have been sold for scrap. So we bought it and built a cooperage around it. After we made our own casks we learned a lot more about wood, like how the

秩父蒸溜所

width of grain affects the quality. Wider grain gives tannin and colour, tighter is more aromatic, so it has been beneficial to us. We might hopefully get local wood this autumn.'

Why, though, take that extra step?

'Why? It's fun! We're whisky enthusiasts, Dave-san, and we want to learn how to make whisky, so that means learn how to make malt, or casks, or plant barley.'

That is very Ichiro. It has to do with whisky-making, for sure, and having some control over parameters, but there is a charitable aspect to this – helping local farmers, or old coopers, hiring the young and enthusiastic who turn up at his door asking for a job. Underlying it all is a desire for understanding of craft and experience – learning from the masters, be they farmers, maltsters, coopers, or other distillers. Now that is whisky-*dō*.

I'm reminded of restaurants like NOMA, where chefs don't only come to do a stage but become involved in the whole process, from the growing of an ingredient to the final dish.

Given this mindset, it would be daft for him not to have a cooperage. I'm tempted to ask if he wants to learn how to make stills, but fear next time there could be a coppersmith down the road as well.

We chat over a tasting. 'Japanese whisky follows Scotch,' he says, 'but even in Scotland the character isn't the same in every distillery. In Japan the variation of temperature creates the character – and the climate is different.

'I can't say "Japanese whisky" because we are making Chichibu. We are pursuing Chichibu character by sticking to an authentic way of making whisky and understanding the minute details that are natural to

Chichibu. We are trying to make the best whisky in the circumstances which we are given.'

'It isn't only one flavour,' adds Yumi, the global brand ambassador. 'The other firms have great technique and don't stick to one flavour – Suntory has never done that. We don't think of one character either. We have to make Chichibu develop. It stands between tradition and development. Some countries only try something new. We respect the tradition, but never stop thinking of the development. That's Japanese, I think.'

On a previous visit Ichiro had said, 'It's only by being here that I have come to appreciate fully the interrelated natural cycle that is needed to make good whisky. It isn't just in the distillery buildings. It's all around us. It's about forestry, and farming as well as distilling. You need all of this' – he'd gestured to the surrounding land – 'to make good whisky.' Maybe that's what nearly 400 years of perspective gives you.

What they are doing has also given a new perspective to Japanese whisky. By taking it back to the land, by re-establishing links with those who grow, malt, dig, and fashion in wood, they are returning Japanese whisky to its long-forgotten roots. It is new, but it is also simultaneously old.

Ichiro and his band of young enthusiasts are showing what possible new approaches could be like, and all of them are rooted in a sense of place, community and old, almost forgotten craftsmanship.

At work in Chichibu's new cooperage.

Chichibu's fame has, rightly, spread internationally, with the result that everyone wants a taste of its whisky. It is, however, a small distillery – and a new one. Ichiro Akuto has to balance the need to keep people interested and happy, while also building up stock for the future. Be patient, though, whisky-lovers; you will be rewarded.

The unpeated new-make is slightly oily, fresh and intense, with just a hint of cereal. Water brings out juicy fruits, blueberry and apple. It sticks to the mouth and doesn't want to leave. The heavy-peated new-make retains the sweetness (now brioche-like) along with smoked apple, woodsmoke and an intriguing wet-wool element. The smoke is strong on the palate, with an added botanical edge.

Single-cask samples give a good idea of how the style(s) is developing. A first-fill American oak cask from 2009 adds its classic vanilla and pine notes to rhubarb and herbs. Water brings out peaches and Japanese clarity and intensity. The palate is filled with spice and juicy yellow fruits.

It wouldn't be Chichibu without some *mizunara* in the mix. A first-fill from 2008 is already picking up *hinoki* and a little incense, backed by a soft, almost buttery/raisin element and those ripe fruits. The tannins are already beginning to shift forward alongside *sanshō*, sweet spices and vanilla. Two years younger, but peated, sees the *mizunara* and the spirit move off in a different direction, the smoke and the richness of the cask adding a new scented element, resinous and haunting.

Of the bottled products, the latest **Chichibu On The Way** from 2015 (55.5% ABV) is a vatting of different vintages and is flagrantly floral (nemesia and ylang-ylang to be precise) with good weight and a touch of icing sugar on the nose. Chichibu's gentle yet assertive clinging quality is there, alongside flowers and white peach and cooked apple. The finish is fresh with decent acidity.

The Peated 2015 (62.5% ABV) was distilled in 2011. It has good depth – that wool note reappears – and a grassy edge along with violet, while there's a *yuzu*-like lift. The palate has a generosity that belies its age. The smoke is in charge at the moment but Chichibu's calm elegance will emerge in time.

A multiplicity of styles is being made.

Ryokan life

Chichibu is a fun town. On the surface it might be a quiet place of hot springs and workaday living that only comes to life at its Night Festival in December, but underneath it's a party town if you know where to look – and if it's whisky you're after, that means Te Airigh (aka 'Terry's bar'), which is where the whole team decants to talk whisky and nonsense, which is, after all, what it is all about.

There's only so much lactobacillus anyone can take, especially when the beer and whisky are flowing and there are more important to discuss with production chief Momma-san, like where to find the best *kani miso* (crab-brain sushi). It's in Hokkaido, apparently, and made from *kegani* (hairy crab). 'You like it?' she looks astonished. 'Let me write it down! You have to try it. It will …' she mimes my head exploding.

The conversation takes a more serious turn as Yumi and I discuss the lack of regulations around Japanese whisky that could allow opportunists to make 'Japanese whisky' of low quality, which then could impact negatively on the whole category. Unlike every other whisky-making country, there is no minimum age statement – allowing new spirit to call itself whisky. Any wood can be used. Neutral spirit can be used in blends. Scotch can be bottled in Japan, be given a smart Japanese label and pass itself off as coming from the country. We are seeing aged rice *shōchū* being sold as Japanese whisky in the U.S.

The reason for this apparent laxity lies in the post-war period when grain was needed for food, therefore whisky-makers had to use different sources. Economically and nutritionally it made sense, but as Yumi points out, while the world has changed, the rules haven't kept pace. In theory, there's nothing to stop a neutral un-aged spirit calling itself Japanese whisky, and with the growth in interest that is a worrying thing.

'Enough,' cries Ichiro. 'There's time for one more round!'

Yumi takes me round to my *ryokan* for the night. There's time for a midnight *onsen* (a hot-spring bath). There's always time for a midnight *onsen*. It gives you time to ease the aches, relax and think.

Ichiro and the team don't say, 'We are making Japanese whisky.' They say, 'We are making whisky in Japan, which by its nature becomes Japanese.' More specifically, they're saying, 'We are making whisky here, which makes it Chichibu.'

Earlier I'd said to Momma-san, 'But you don't have to plough and harvest, and dig peat.' She'd looked momentarily nonplussed. 'Why not? It is how you learn, and if you learn by practice, you are better at judging the fine details.'

Is it as simple as attention to detail? You can't say Scotland doesn't have that. Maybe here it's the nature of their joined-up whisky thinking and a deep relationship with the landscape. It's using your conditions and aligning them with those of other craftspeople.

Whisky-*dō* isn't an empty phrase; it is about learning, and listening, and doing. It isn't that the team cares more; it's that the care it has manifests itself in a slightly different way because of the location and the conditions. That's what's wrong with the reductive 'who is better?' argument. The Japanese simply try to make the best Japanese whisky they can.

I hit the futon and fall asleep immediately. It has been a gorgeous day.

SHIBUI

I should tell you about the cup. As we neared Chichibu, Take decided that he should try and get some 'foggy mountain' shots, so we turned off the highway and took the first road that looked as if it might be heading uphill. We corkscrewed through dripping woods and rain-slicked old steps, past a tiny shrine, houses, a strange-looking astronomical observatory. Parked up, we headed into the woods, slithering about in the rain, as the drops battered the leaves. I sheltered in a hut and looked across the valley as Take headed further towards what was now clearly a cliff edge. He returned soon after, wiping his head with a towel. The clouds were still too low for the perfect effect, but I had realized by now that he is an eternal optimist. 'If it's a dull day, it's a dull day,' he said. 'The photos will be the truth!'

We headed back downhill, but rather than rejoining the main road, Ogachi began travelling down a succession of narrow country lanes, the rain stirring up the mud in the paddy fields, our car startling a duck which flew off in great irritation.

He pulled up in the driveway of someone's house. I figured he was lost and asking for directions. Instead, he said, 'OK. Lunch,' and headed towards the back door. I could see no sign, but followed, into a tiny soba restaurant.

The greatest meals are the simplest. Crisp and delicate tempura, cold noodles made from local buckwheat to be dipped into a deep and intense duck broth. A sign on the wall said that the set lunch could include a glass of Ichiro's malt. 'He eats here,' we were told with pride. It seemed rude not to take advantage of the offer.

It came in a rough-textured ceramic cup, slightly irregular, with a red glaze striping the surface and a bluish blister on the inside. Made by the chef's father, it was so right, so humble. It held the local whisky sitting next to the local soba and a broth quite probably made from the duck's partner. This little understated cup had *shibui*.

This is one of those slippery aesthetic terms, like *wabi-sabi*, which are integral to Japanese craft but are almost impossible to translate. Objects which have *shibui* are 'quiet', and deep. They aren't in any way showy or glitzy. Instead there is a simplicity, a lack of decoration.

For Soetsu Yanagi, the philosopher behind the 20th-century revival of interest in traditional craft,

shibui 'is not a beauty displayed before the viewer by its creator; creation here means ... making a piece that will lead the viewer to draw beauty out of it for himself ... in *shibui*, beauty is beauty that makes an artist of the viewer ... It is modest, restrained, and inward-looking [with] simple naturalness.'

I've long believed that whisky (like all drinks in fact) doesn't exist in a bubble outside the culture from which it springs. It has a cultural terroir and the needs, desires, and framework that drove its creation, be they aesthetic or philosophical, will affect it. Whisky isn't simply created by process and moulded by climate; it is the product of a mindset, and that mindset is at its root cultural rather than commercial. It is inextricably linked to the place and the people. If you want to try and grasp what makes Japanese whisky Japanese, then there has to be an examination of these links – and one is *shibui*.

I'm now not only tasting differently, with thoughts of the arc of maturity and its relation to seasons, but whether whiskies can exhibit qualities such as *shibui*. 'The plain and unagitated,' Yanagi writes in *The Unknown Craftsman* (2013), '... the natural, the innocent, the humble, the modest, where does beauty lie if not in these qualities? The meek, the austere, the un-ornate – they are the national characteristics that gain man's affection and respect.'

Think of the whiskies and their transparency. Those aromas that are intense but delicate, which never shout, which have calm and modesty, naturalness and quiet depth. That cup had it; the whisky does as well.

I wrote to Yumi asking if she could ask the father if I could possibly buy one. A few weeks later a package arrived. In it was 'my' cup as a gift from him. I'm looking at it now.

Humble, modest, restrained – keys to *shibui*.

MIZUNARA

Japanese whiskies can differentiate themselves from other styles by a number of methods: clear wort, distillation techniques, the influence of climate. In terms of aromatics, the use of Japanese oak (*mizunara*) can also have a significant impact, adding an extra layer of exoticism to the whole aromatic spectrum.

While *mizunara* (*mizu* means water, *nara* means oak) grows across eastern Asia, Siberia, Sakhalin and the Kuril Islands, it's rare in Japan. Though found across northern Honshu, its main stronghold was in Hokkaido, but as settlers began to spread across the northern island from the start of the Meiji era (1876), they cleared the primeval forest in order to create pasture.

A type of white oak, *Quercus crispula*, it is slow growing – a tree can take up to 150 years to reach maturity – with a wide grain. While still used for flooring, furniture and household utensils, *mizunara* has never been the cooper's friend. Prone to having knots, this type of wood is also low in tyloses, a substance that blocks the pores of the tree's heartwood and makes a cask watertight.

It was only used by the Japanese whisky industry in the Second World War because there was no supply of oak from America. During the post-war reconstruc-tion, supplies of American oak started up afresh, and *mizunara* casks fell from favour.

Its revival is solely down to its remarkable aromatic qualities. Over time, it adds aromas of scented woods such as sandalwood and cedar, but most significantly the smell of aloeswood, which is used as the base for the incense burned in Japanese temples. You can also pick out a camphor mintiness with occasional autumnal notes of leaves, earth and coconut; this last comes from cis- and trans-lactone. The oak also appears to intensify the acidity of the whisky, adding a brightness to it. Often too intense to be bottled on its own, *mizunara* casks are valuable weapons for a blender making a complex single malt or a blend.

Suntory holds the largest stock of casks and is coopering a small amount every year, replanting more trees for every one that is felled. Every other distiller, bar Nikka, however, is using it, albeit in small quantities.

Mizunara (on the right) has a different structure to American oak (on the left), which makes it hard to cooper.

Chichibu to Tokyo

I rise early, heaving myself in ungainly fashion from floor to upright. My room has an outside tub filled constantly by the hot spring. I wash, then soak, write some notes, then do it all again. An *onsen* cleans the skin and the mind somehow. You leave tingling, ready for the world again. Maybe breakfast—multicourse, homemade, tiny dishes of pickles and fish, rice porridge and miso soup. Can I really have a third soak before leaving? The old wooden floor creaks. There's time. Birdsong comes across from the trees on the opposite bank, the bamboo shade shimmers in the rippling water. And at that point the sun comes out and the water splits into gold.

Yumi picks me up to take me to the station and the direct train back to Tokyo, through steep-sided, forested gorges, flashes of wild garlic, dull red tree trunks, and just outside Koma, a white crane in a green rice field; isolated farms, tiny plots of people making do as their ancestors had made do for centuries. We rattle down the track, away from the idyll and back to the hungry chaos of the city. It's balance, I try to convince myself. At least I was clean, ready for it.

I check in to my home at the Park Hotel and call Take. 'It's time to hit some bars.'

TOKYO BAR LIFE

ZOETROPE

If you really want to geek out on Scotch, head to Campbelltoun Loch, but as that's not the remit, the must-visit bar for anyone interested in 'Japanese-distilled, Western-style spirits' is Zoetrope in Shinjuku.

It's run by former movie exec and Hawaiian-shirt aficionado Horigami-san. There are silent movies playing on a large screen and a selection of soundtracks (on vinyl of course) to play as an accompaniment. Behind the stick, the shelves are crammed with the greatest selection of 'Japanese-distilled ... etc., etc.' obscurities you'll ever see. If you want to understand the truths about Japanese whisky, this is the place to come.

The bar opened in 2006, almost as a home for a collection of obscurities Horigami had started to gather in the mid-1990s. So what was the motivation? 'I'm a bit like like the 1950s generation. I didn't have money, imported whiskies were expensive, so I began drinking Japanese. Back then I didn't appreciate flavour.'

Jota Tanaka joins us as, glass by glass, we begin to tease out the facts behind the Japanese whisky boom.

That boom may have been built on blends, but they weren't all of the status of, say, Hibiki. It was the time of Suntory's Torys and Kakubin, Nikka's Red, and many more. These were low-cost, often low-strength, mass-market brands sold at prices which the whisky-drinking working man could afford. Indeed, the domestic tax system ensured that this would be the case.

From 1940 until 1989, the industry operated a three-tier system. Whisky was either special grade (bottled at 43% ABV), first grade (40% ABV), or second grade (37% ABV). The lower the malt content, the lower the grade – and the tax. Those second-tier whiskies were deliberately aimed at people with low incomes.

What could be used as the non-malt portion was eye-openingly wide-ranging. As well as what we would regard as whisky – distilled, grain-based spirit – 'whisky' could also be made 'by distilling alcoholic substances made from germinated grain and other materials, provided that, if the alcoholic substance is made from a mixture of materials containing germinated grain and fruits, the weight of the germinated grain is greater than that of the fruits ... and liquors produced by adding alcohol, spirits, *shochu*, flavouring, colouring or water

to whisky malt and whose flavour, colour, and other properties are similar to those of whisky malt.' It's not the 'Japanese whisky' we've been experiencing in recent years.

We're sipping some of the second-grade whiskies. Nikka's Northlands – 'meant for Highball' says the label – is bland, grain-heavy, and tastes like a mix of green beans and sugar. Ocean, the parent firm of Karuizawa, is hefty and oily, like drinking chewing gum and pear drops, while the same firm's White Ship ('white whisky, Canadian type') has the same gummy quality, but with more vanilla extract.

In addition, imported spirits were taxed at a higher rate again. In 1986, the EU complained to the World Trade Organisation that this system was unfairly discriminatory. Three years later, the old grading system was scrapped and import duties scrapped.

Scotch prices fell and began to compete with the domestic brands, with the first- and second-grade whiskies the hardest hit. 'Nineteen eighty-nine was the moment when things changed,' says Horigami, pulling out some more bottles. 'The quality had to be upped.'

He pours us some Mars Rare Old Blended (from the Yamanashi distillery), sweet on the nose, light, fruity

and balanced; and Golden Horse 8-year-old single malt from Hanyu (bottled at 39% ABV) sweet (what is it with the sugar?) and smelling of toffee, miso and vegetables.

Though single malts and higher-quality blends were growing, the 1990s were also when Japanese whisky hit the buffers. Part of it might have been down to the changes in tax. The knock-on effects of the Asian financial crisis undoubtedly had an impact, as did the simple fact that there was a generation reaching drinking age who didn't want to sit all night in *izakayas* knocking back *mizuwaris* (whisky, ice and water) like their fathers and grandfathers had.

This resulted in some remarkable attempts to regain credibility and reach out to the young – always a dangerous thing when the ones who are making the decisions are middle-aged executives. We get a flight of dad-dancing drams: Suntory's Rawhide, a 40% ABV blend of bourbon and Japanese whisky that smells like the set of *Happy Days*, all menthol and bubblegum. Kirin-Seagram's NEWS 500 ('design-taste-life') with a fantastic label design and glass, that mixes choco-

Atsushi Origami, guardian of Japan's whisky past.

latey butterscotch, fat corn and flowers; then the same distiller's Hips, 'the brightest whiskey' with a slightly risqué label of a flapper girl popping a flask down her stocking top. Back came Suntory with the spirity Q1000, 'light and smooth' in an odd canister-shaped green bottle, and branded glass considerably less cool than the NEWS one.

'NEWS was the moment things changed,' recalls Jota, 'The firm was making 100-per-cent-authentic whisky, but with no regulations, anything went!' The bottles pile up. Kirin's Saturday, 'high-quality whisky for the new age' and Suntory's attempt to attract a hip new crowd with the Smokey & Co series, Natural Mellow, Super Smokey and Fine Mint. The latter is, er, minty but the whisky is balanced and would make a good instant julep.

Sales continued to fall along with prices, but the inventory piled up. 'Our Evermore 21-year-old was Y10,000 [c.£70],' recalls Jota. Horigami finds a bottle of Karuizawa 25-year-old from the same era.

'This, though, was a turning point,' he says, bringing out a bottle with a delicate watercolour strip of a label: Suntory's Pure Malt from the Southern Alps. If the nation's palate had gone to *shochu*, here was a

whisky to try and wean it back – perfumed, sugary and light. That didn't work either.

There is, of course, a flipside to this. Some people who know about the pre-1989 landscape assume that everything made before this was poor, which isn't true. There were great whiskies in those days; the market was just more varied, and led by the bottom end.

To prove the former point we finish with proper glasses of Ichiro's bottling for Kyosato Field Ballet's 26th anniversary: an immense savoury, leathery blend of Hanyu 1992 and Kawasaki 1982. Not everything was light and sweet.

The Japanese industry wasn't forced to make better whiskies in 1989. Instead, the changes in the rules simply gave the whisky-makers greater incentive to continue what had been happening already, the exploration of the top end, innovation and the refusal to accept the job was complete.

It's only thanks to people like Horigami-san that this now half-forgotten story can be told.

'Dad-dancing' whiskies of the 1990s.

HISASHI KISHI

You cannot deny that Hisashi Kishi has presence. His main bar (he has two in Ginza and one in Kyoto), Star Bar, is the only one I will always go to on every visit to Tokyo, just to sit and watch him work. He's been the International Bartenders Association's world champion, heads the Nippon Bartenders Association, and is a TV star. The perfect person to explain some of the finer points of how to craft a cocktail the Japanese way.

Japanese bars tend to be small and crepuscular. The whisky selection will be huge, the glassware antique, the music cool jazz. The drinks will take time. Making one – be it water, beer, a neat whisky, or a cocktail will be done with precision and care.

That is what Kishi-san represents. Initially reserved, the laughs soon come, the stories increasingly discursive. I wanted to talk to him about shaking before he started his evening shift. I've watched him do it for years, moving as if he is doing a karate kata: nothing wasted, every move fluid and purposeful. This isn't shake as show, this is shake as part of a philosophy.

We get to it eventually after a long chat about the roots of Japanese bartending and the now-forgotten generation who started it all. 'I don't think that we Japanese have a traditional method in terms of bartending, so there is no innovation either. You know what they say: we can't invent a car but we can improve on it,' is his opening gambit.

But things have changed, surely? 'At the end of the Showa era (1980s) there was a video made of some masters who were about to pass away, making cocktails. When you look at it, the method is different to now.'

Japan's conditions also had a part to play in the evolution of the style. 'Not many bars had air conditioning in the old days,' he says, 'and Japan is so humid, so the ice melts. For example, when the Palace Hotel opened for the Olympics in 1964, there were no electric fridges, just an icebox. Kiyoshi Imai was the head bartender – he was a legend – and he just put the gin in there as well. In my time [with fridges] I still put the gin for Martinis in the fridge as well. In many ways it is Japan's conditions that have created the shake.'

Japan is known as the repository of traditional bartending skills. Techniques are used here which have almost disappeared elsewhere in the world. Kishi's

Hisashi Kishi, godfather of Japanese bartending.

point is that these are not, as many people think, Japanese inventions, but adaptations.

'In Japan we try to look at the origins of something and try to stay true to it. We feel a great respect for tradition, but also we change it.' There's that seeming paradox again. You ask about a 'Japanese' way, but there are lots of ways that might affect it: culture, climate, the land. It is the same for whisky.

What, though, of the traditional master/student relationship, which can be seen in bars, or the fact that the NBA seems to be a more significant player in setting standards than in other countries? 'The fact that we had the NBA meant there was a large community and a lot of exchange of information. Many things were learned in that way. At the same time, though, there are pitfalls with that. When you say that something has to be done in a specific way, the base level becomes higher, but it can become restrictive.'

It's an oblique admission that some aspects of this control of tradition can stifle innovation. From personal experience that might have been the case, but with more Japanese bartenders travelling internationally and western bartenders visiting Japan there is a new generation with a wider concept of making drinks – while always retaining the key aspects of service and technique. It is not inflexible.

The most visible of these has been Hidetsugu Ueno, former student of Kishi-san and owner of Ginza's Bar High Five, which has become the first stop for most international bartenders visiting Tokyo. These days, Ueno seems to spend almost as much time on the road as he does behind the bar. His message is a subtle one. He may teach the classicism that underpins the 'Japanese approach', but does so in an amusingly self-deprecating way, understanding that its conservatism is both an asset and a drawback.

In Tokyo, Ueno takes the knowledge he has gleaned from his friends in the world's best bars, or from observing what competitors are doing in international competitions, and applies it to those founding principles. Like its whisky, Japanese bartending cannot stand still, it must be as fluid as the shake.

The conversation has moved on to ice. 'I see ice as an ingredient,' says Kishi-san. 'I want it to be involved, to add texture and be part of the process. If you use a metal shaker and hard ice and shake in a specific way you will get fine bubbles, and foaming, and that adds texture.'

He moves behind the bar and demonstrates. The shaker becomes an extension of his body, held at eye level, moving fluidly, with grace, everything controlled by the hands cupping it in a specific grip, moving the shaker towards himself, then away, upside down, then back again. There is none of the 'Look at me, I'm making a drink' that you see in Western bars. He shakes for a specific reason.

'In a short shake like this, you get a lot of control of the ice. It is slow enough to allow it to flow around inside. The cubes aren't bashing together. It's not like this!' He slaps his face. 'It's to do with the amount of dilution it gives while flowing around the liquid.' He pours the ice out like poker dice. The edges are smooth. 'You see? Ice shaped like that will move in a different way.' He grins.

He has been using a small, three-part shaker. Does the size of the shaker have an effect? 'When you are cooking, you use a frying pan for some things, and different-sized pans for others. It depends on what you are cooking.

'A Boston shaker [the tall shaker consisting of a mixing glass and a metal tin] is not good or bad, right or wrong. It is what it is. It allows for more volume and because the metal side is grooved with one straight side the ice moves about less, but goes back and forward.

'You can't make the same drink in a different shaker. That's what Western bartenders don't understand. They come here and learn the technique, then go back and use a different shaker. It's not technique; it is what you use.

'For 100 years we had this attitude of "not better, but different", and it takes time to recognize those differences. We take things seriously. Our way of doing things is a build-up of details but we want to do the right thing at the base. Japanese style is thinking about details. You change little bits. In the West it's just process.' He laughs again. He knows the world is listening.

Kishi-san's shaking technique is like watching a karate kata.

TAKAYUKI SUZUKI

I have known Takayuki Suzuki since I first started visiting Japan, mainly thanks to the fact that he is in charge of the bars at the Park Hotel and Shiba Park. He has been provider of drinks, counsellor, hospitable host and a solicitous friend. His book, *The Perfect Martini*, is a must-read.

He is also one of the deepest thinkers about bartending that I know. Sit with him at one of his bars and you meet someone who is part-psychologist, part-therapist and part-shaman. When he still tended the bars he would slide a drink over to you. 'I hope you like this,' is all he would say. You'd ask for the ingredients and then its name. 'That's up to you. I've just made it up because I think it suits your mood.' You sipped it. Boom – he had done it again. He'd smile gently and step back, almost into the shadows.

It's normal for a visitor to take the straight-back, hands-clasped-in-front stance of the Japanese bartender as reticence. There are few – Horigami at Zoe-trope, Yamashita-san at Three Martini, Hidetsugu Ueno at the legendary High Five – who break the fourth wall and become more involved, but even there, there will

be a relationship established with you as the customer and them as the bartender. It's called service.

Imagine this scenario. Three of us walk into a bar. One of us wants a beer, the other a glass of water, and I'll have a cocktail. In the West, the cocktail will be laboured over, the beer quickly poured, the water possibly forgotten and sent over as an afterthought. In Japan, each of these drinks will be served with the same care and attention – the best drink that the bartender can make at that moment: right glassware, right temperature, right presentation.

It's an example of the concept of *ichi-go ichi-e*: 'one time, one meeting, one encounter' which, thanks to the work of international bartender Stan Vadrna and Nikka, is becoming more appreciated outside Japan. The bartender has only one chance to make you welcome, to make you comfortable, to give you the best drink he can at that moment. Right concentration, right mindfulness, right speech, right thought, right action.

We sit at the bar at the Park and chat this over. 'In this way, the bartender isn't the hero. He has to ask what kind of taste do you like, what's going on, how are you? Check the mood. The drink is more important than the bartender.'

It extends to his approach to whisky. 'Scotch has strong advance flavour, so you can recognize its character very quickly. Japanese whisky is very quiet: "Come on…wake up!" When I taste it, I prefer two glasses, one straight and one a wine glass and roll between the two. That movement helps me find the secret of flavour.'

So, that quietness. It has *shibui*? 'Yes. And the approach is about respect for the object. It is "Look at me, I am the hero". It's the same with ice.'

Again, though, Western bartenders – and drinkers – get caught up with technique and the tools. It's like with whisky; the obsession with size, shape, numbers distracts you from what matters: flavour. To accentuate the role of ice, he builds his drinks from that element up. 'Crushed ice allows you to drink alcohol at extra-low temperature, so it is perfect for a summer drink when it is humid. People will ask for a "Yamazaki Mist" as that's what happens to the glass.'

So the seasons are important? 'We have to know what kind of food to find in the four or five days of that "season" and that means the bartender has to change the taste of the cocktail. Beginning of spring is good for Hakushu; the end of autumn is Yamazaki 18 – at the

beginning it would be on an ice ball as you still need to cool down a little.'

Ah. The ice ball. The symbol of Japanese bartending. In every bar you will hear the tinkling of shards of ice being chipped away. You can now buy ice-ball moulds so you can do it at home.

That's missing the point. The ice ball isn't there for show; it is there for a reason. 'If I could make a better drink by throwing a bottle, I'd do it,' Kishi had said to me earlier with a giant laugh. 'But you don't see sushi chefs spinning fish, do you?'

The ice ball allows the whisky to be cooled and very slightly diluted, but for Suzuki there are other layers. There always are. 'A long time ago, in the times of the shoguns, ice was a gift to powerful people; it was government-controlled. Only the elite could eat ice, and therefore the image of ice is a symbol of power. Its quality is a sign of hospitality.

'A design concept is good if it is close to nature,' he continues. 'In *kaiseki*, for example, the concept is a mountain, because the mountain makes snow, the snow makes the river, the water gives food, then it

An ice ball is more than decoration.

becomes the ocean, which gives us fish, and then it rises and forms clouds that fall on the mountain. In *kaiseki* the food arrangement will have a sunny side and a shadow side, just like the mountain. So do my garnishes.

'The ice ball is a stone on a riverbank that has been turned by the water, so the ice ball talks about time, its shape is representative of time. It's not technique, or design; it is a philosophy of Japanese identity.'

And with that he says his goodbye, the quiet philosopher of mixed drinks who looks further into flavour than most. Head spinning slightly, I get in the lift and to bed.

Bartender as philosopher: Takayuki Suzuki.

Bar Hopping

Jota heads home, while Take and I wander down to Shinjuku's 'Piss Alley' (to give it its nickname) seeking something to eat – or maybe drink. Bar Albatross, whose ground floor is a velvet-lined shoebox with dangling chandeliers, is a logical stop. Upstairs there's more seating, and you order your drink by opening a hatch in the floor. On one previous visit, a very drunken physicist fell through and was only saved by being grabbed round his armpits. 'You'd think he of all people would understand gravity,' said one of my companions. It's rammed, though, so we walk through the fug of *yakitori* grill smoke to a steam-filled noodle bar and load up on slippery udon and greasy broth – and a couple of Nikka Highballs.

'Golden Gai?' I suggest. Clearly the food has worked. We stroll on. One minute your eyeballs are being dazzled by the lights of Kabukicho, the next you're plunged into a hidden, darkened maze of alleyways crammed full of minuscule bars. Golden Gai is Tokyo's underground, a place on the margins that plays by its own rules.

You don't go to Golden Gai to find great whisky bars. You come here to talk, to enter a forgotten demimonde and to create that mood, one bottle is quite sufficient. You also have to find the right bar. The one that suits your sensibilities on that night, *ichi-go ichi-e*.

Some say that these days Golden Gai simply panders to the tourist trade by offering a sanitized version of old Tokyo. Some establishments may do that, but a bar owner once said to me, 'We're not preserving anything; we're simply running our bars the way we want to. Until you are invited into this bar you think it's closed to outsiders.' But surely it is? She smiled. 'To a certain extent. You need an introduction, but for all who come in maybe 20 per cent will stay as regulars.' So the bars are manifestations of the owner's personality? 'Indeed. The customers are people who have the same...tendency, talent, thoughts.'

I've sat in publishers' bars, or listened to free jazz in silence, in others, I've watched old movies, or found one where you could only discuss hard-boiled fiction. Every niche is covered here. This used to be a red-light district. Some bars have an upper deck where the girls used to ply their trade. Golden Gai has somehow survived in a city that is in a permanent state of renewal. This is partly thanks to no single landlord owning the block, allowing this anarchic, egalitarian, bohemian quarter to remain a place of refuge for like-minded outsiders. 'It is like an island in Tokyo without being in Tokyo,' said the owner of the hard-boiled fiction bar to me. 'We're the Independent City of Golden Gai!'

Take chose the dinner location so it's my choice for the bar, which is surprisingly hard, given there are 270 to choose from. I can't find the hard-boiled bar; the sherry one is great, I know, but not tonight. We turn a corner and there's a door with a psychedelic painting on it. That's more like it.

The owner has been there for 40 years. 'I used to put gigs on here,' he says, pouring our drinks. We look at him in disbelief. He shows us photos of a guy perched on a platform above the bar with a guitar, the audience of ten (the place was full) craning their necks to see.

'Look upstairs. I've got seats there now.' We clamber up, surprising an already well-relaxed group. 'Don't worry,' says Take. 'He's a whisky writer,' as if that will explain everything. 'Wow! We'll all buy the book! Have a drink!'

Downstairs, a drunken Austrian is contemplating how he can get home. We have another. I rush for the subway and get the last train to Shimbashi. Tomorrow will be a different sort of bar. I need a clear head.

These we have lost

Think of them as collateral damage. Whisky can be brutal. It gets caught up in the eddies of economics and changing taste. Sometimes it can steer itself free but not all distilleries make it. Every whisky-making country has its ghost sites where spirit once ran and men crafted. Japan is no different. Here are some of those we have lost.

We've already heard of Hombo's Yamanashi distillery, where Iwai's vision finally manifested itself, and of the firm's short-lived distillery at Kagoshima.

Shirakawa in Fukushima is no more. Purchased post-war by Takara Shuzou (owner of Scotland's Tomatin distillery) it supplied malt for the King blend. It closed in 2003 after a period in mothballs, another victim of the downturn.

Grain whisky was affected as well. In 1935, a distillery in Kawasaki began making industrial alcohol. Owned by brewer Showa Shuzo (later Sanraku Shuzo), it began making malt whisky in the 1950s, though it became best known as a grain distillery that ran from the late 1960s until its closure. Guess when? In the mid-1980s. Ichiro Akuto acquired the last remaining casks.

In 1961, Showa bought another distiller called Ocean (whose whiskies we tried at Zoetrope; see page 94) the distilling arm of a wine producer called Daikoku Budoshu (aka Mercian), which had been producing wine in Yamanashi since the late 19th century. In 1939, Daikoku opened another winery at the spa town of Karuizawa, which sits under Japan's most active volcano, Mount Asama. Keen to enter the post-war whisky market, Daikoku launched the Ocean brand in 1946 and built its first distillery in Shiojiri, Nagano prefecture, in 1952. The quality from Shiojiri was poor and so a decision was taken to close it down and change Karuizawa from a winery to a distillery. Spirit ran from its stills from 1956 until 2000.

Those stills were small, peated Golden Promise barley was used, and the spirit went into Sherry casks. Everything about Karuizawa was built around muscle and power in order to give structure and weight to the Ocean blends. Only towards the end of its life did Mercian (as Showa/ Sanraku was known by then) consider it might be released as a single malt.

In 2006, the firm was bought by Kirin. It seemed the perfect match: Gotemba's light elegance and Karuizawa's power. Kirin seemed set to challenge the duopoly of Suntory and Nikka. Instead, the brewer closed the site, sold off the land and returned the distilling licence, a decision that remains baffling. The only positive was that the 300 remaining casks were bought by Number One Drinks. Karuizawa survived in the strange half-life of a silent still. At least we could drink it. It tasted earthy, feral, sooty but also of resin, old churches and deep forests, concentrated fruits and rice crackers. Bold.

The stock was stored at Chichibu. Ichiro Akuto knew all about closed distilleries. His family firm, Toa Shuzo, had been distilling at Hanyu since 1941, though whisky (Golden Horse) only started in the early 1980s. Bigger, slightly drier than standard Japanese malts of the time, it proved to be a hard sell in the *mizuwari* market. In 2000, Toa Shuzo filed for bankruptcy and was sold to a sake and *shochu* producer. The distillery was dismantled in 2004.

Thankfully, with backing from sake brewer Sasanokawa Shuzo (see page 109) Akuto managed to buy back the Hanyu stock, which was then released in a number of guises: vattings with other distilleries, on its own, and as part of the 'Card Series'. The market had shifted.

The unwanted Hanyu and Karuizawa styles were now in line with people's palates, but ultimately only some people's pockets. The limited nature of the latter's releases meant that prices rose and rose to eye-watering levels. The whiskies now exist in the realm of the speculator, not the whisky-lover.

Cognitive dissonance can descend when a distillery closes. Critical faculties become dulled, and any flaws or faults are ignored because the whisky is rare. The fear of the finite induces panic. I was fortunate enough to taste those 300 Karuizawa casks. There were some amazing whiskies, but plenty which were overextracted. These were never intended as single-malt bottlings. Sherry casks were used to balance the weight of the spirit and also to add tannin, because that's what a blend required. Some were simply left for too long.

It is best to remember Karuizawa as it was at its best, and should we raise a glass of it, or Hanyu, think of the web of chance and fortune that dictates whisky's fortunes.

As the *haiku* poet Issa wrote:
.腹中は誰も浅間のけぶり哉
fukuchû wa dare mo asama no keburi kana

deep inside
of everyone, Mount Asama's
smoke

These we are gaining

It is frustrating enough for a Japanese whisky-lover that stock is in short supply. What was more surprising on this trip, given the boom in distillery-building globally, was how few new distilleries were starting up. Thankfully things have now changed. Here is a roundup of what is happening and about to happen.

The furthest north of the new-builds is in Akkeshi on the east coast of Hokkaido. Owned by food importer Kenten, it is aiming to produce 100,000 litres a year. The bulk of production will be of a heavily peated style (the malt comes from Crisp). It follows a classic Japanese approach with clear wort and very long (four-day) ferments. Different yeasts are being trialled. One of the stills has a similar plain pear shape to Lagavulin, which encourages reflux. A wide variety of casks are being used, with *mizunara* intended to be a focus.

The first question about Akkeshi is the one I would have asked Taketsuru: why Hokkaido? The answer, from distiller Clint Anesbury, was similar. 'Akkeshi's environment is similar to Islay in climate, terrain and maritime qualities, not to mention the rich abundance of available peat.' In fact it was the peat that was the clincher. That implies that the plans are to use it. 'In the long term we plan to produce a 100 per cent Akkeshi single-malt whisky using local barley, peat and *mizunara* from local forests.'

While its approach is slightly different to Akkeshi, Islay was also the inspiration for a new distillery in the mountains to the north of Shizuoka, as managing director Taiko Nakamura explained. 'In 2012, I travelled to Islay and Jura. The final distillery of my tour was Kilchoman. The site was so small and their technology was old-fashioned. It was there I got an idea to build my own micro-distillery in Japan.'

Shizuoka will be making between 70,000 and 250,000 litres a year, and while initially all the malt (peated and unpeated) will be UK-sourced, Japanese barley is being planned. Ferments are, like Akkeshi, very long – up to 138 hours.

There are three stills. Two are from Forsyths in Speyside, the third is one of the old stills from Karuizawa. One of the Forsyths stills is direct-fired. The model, it would seem, is as much Springbank as Kilchoman. 'I want to try distillation in various ways,' says Nakamura. 'Double, and partial triple. I want this to be a new style in Japanese whisky.'

A lot further south on Kyushu is Hombo's new plant in Tsunuki, close to Kagoshima, which will be making initially 108,000 litres a year from unpeated, lightly and heavily peated UK-sourced malt. The firm will be using dried, beer and its own yeast strains for the four-day ferment. 'Tsunuki is where Hombo Shuzo was founded back in 1872,' says the firm's Haruna Waki. 'Also whisky made and aged in Kagoshima could contain some hints that make people think, "I can imagine that the southern islands have made this whisky".' Ageing is taking place at Tsunuki and further south in Yakushima. 'We expect our whisky matures faster than it does in Mars Shinshu. So we want our new-make to be full-bodied, not to take too much cask flavour.'

At the time of writing the new Yonezawa distillery in Akashi is operating with a single Forsyths pot still, with a second arriving later in the year. Temperature-controlled fermenters are being used, as is a mix of woods.

Another distillery has re-opened. Sasanokawa Shuzo has been a sake brewer for 251 years and distilled from 1945 to 1988. (As well as owning the Cherry whisky brand, it was the firm which helped Ichiro Akuto buy his Hanyu stock, and distributed the initial releases). Now it has re-opened its Asaka distillery in Koriyama, Fukushima Prefecture, complete with new pot stills.

In addition there is also whisky-making at the multifunctional Kiuchi brewery in Ibaraki Prefecture (it makes sake, beer, *shochu* and wine). Its whisky distillery, Nukada, is being run by Sam Yoneda with former Suntory master blender Seiichi Koshimizu as consultant. Expect some cross-fertilization between the craft beer and whisky-making sides.

Miyashita Shuzo, based in Okayama, is another firm with experience in other liquor styles – it is best known these days as a craft brewer. Whisky-making was therefore a logical extension. A Holstein still is used and there is also a heavy reliance on local Sky Golden barley. Up to half of the distillery's requirements is Japanese-grown. Currently they distil once a week. (My thanks to the *Malt Whisky Yearbook 2017* for the information on the last two distilleries.)

The whisky world they are entering is considerably different to that which put paid to distilleries from the 1980s onwards. All are making single malt rather than blends, all are looking locally as well and all are following what is now established as a Japanese approach to whisky distillation.

'In my opinion it goes beyond just materials,' said Anesbury. 'Perhaps what makes Japanese whisky different, especially in the production, is the need for perfection. Many craftsmen in Japan often treat their job as an art, and where there are artisans there are differences – differences of detail.'

The most pressing issue isn't making the whisky but having a regulatory framework that stops firms from importing alcohol, bottling it in Japan and selling it as Japanese whisky, or mixing 90 per cent neutral alcohol with malt spirit and calling it whisky. A minimum time maturing in cask is also required.

The arrival of new distillers shows that the door is open for new, quality-oriented producers. Unfortunately it is so wide open that chancers can flow through as well. A proper regulatory system is urgently needed..

The New York Bar, Park Hyatt Tokyo
(following pages).

Chita

知多蒸溜所

Tokyo to Chita

It is time to quit Tokyo and head west. First stop, Nagoya, which, though Japan's fourth-largest city, is not high on most people's tour agendas. No-one seems to go to Nagoya for the sights. Very few, I think it fair to say, go there for its whisky. In fact, not many people even know there's whisky from the greater Nagoya district, but if you think in terms of volume there's actually more made here than anywhere else – and it comes from one distillery, Chita.

We head by *shinkansen* (bullet train) to Nagoya, where things slow down considerably as we take a small local service that rattles along the spit of land which hooks around from Nagoya like a dragon's claw. There's no sightseeing to be done here. We're on the edgelands of the city, surrounded by docks, industrial sites and shipyards. It's good to get some balance. After a weekend of shrines and fine bars, *ukiyo-e* (woodblock prints) galleries, quiet parks and sushi this is an important recalibration. Whisky isn't always made in the rural hideaways I'd seen in that first week. Sometimes it is industrial and urban, large-scale and, for some, ugly.

I like grain distilleries. Yes, I know there's not the romance of pot stills, and they look different, but industrial architecture has its own brutal beauty, much of which comes from its scale. Take and I stand outside the site, dwarfed by it. 'Wide-angle lens today,' he grins.

The impersonal nature of a grain distillery, the look of the equipment, are things from which whisky firms are usually keen to divert your gaze. Best keep whisky cuddly and warm, with fat-bellied pots, and landscape, not columns and pipework and vast levels of production. Yet, without understanding grain and scale you cannot get to grips with the size of the industry.

Japan was built on blends and blends are built on grain. Welcome to whisky reality.

The brutal beauty of Chita's fermenters.

CHITA

My guide today is Hisashi Maemura, another of Suntory's seemingly endless chain of jolly, perfectly turned-out whisky-makers. Put it this way: not many people can make a hard hat look like a fashion statement. We head straight to the massive curves of the grain silos. Take and I hang back as Maemura walks towards them, becoming increasingly dwarfed by their bulk.

Built in 1972, the distillery is a 50:50 joint venture between Suntory and Zen-Noh, the giant (it would have to be) federation of over 1,000 agricultural co-ops whose business includes everything from grain imports, animal feeds and fertilizers, all the way to tractors, Wagyu beef and the Tokimeite restaurant in London.

It made sound commercial sense. With the domestic whisky market in substantial growth, Suntory needed its own supply of grain whisky while Zen-Noh was in the process of expanding its reach. The location was logical as well. While Chita might not be most people's idea of a seaside distillery, building it next to an existing grain-unloading dock was logical. The corn comes from Canada and the US, while the malted barley used by the distillery is a six-row strain from Finland best suited to the process. The distillery is, perhaps unsurprisingly, the biggest such operation in the country.

The four silos are split between corn and malted barley, samples of both being taken to check for grain size, water content and overall quality before processing.

While the equipment certainly looks nothing like a malt distillery, essentially the same principle applies here as in malt production. You have a grain which you convert into a liquid containing fermentable sugars which you then ferment and distil. All that's different is the grain, the techniques – and the scale.

There's no mash tun in a grain distillery. Instead we wander to a set of six 25-m-long (82-foot) horizontal pipes. In fact, it's just a single one coiled like a massive anaconda. This, Maemura explains, is where the cooking and conversion takes place. In the lowest level of the pipes, the mix of corn and water (which is pumped in as there's no natural source on site) is heated to 70°C (158ºF), then raised to 150°C (302ºF) to soften the kernel. The liquid slurry is then pumped up to a tower where the temperature is dropped to 100°C (212ºF) before it flows back into the tube. Now at 60-65°C (140°-149ºF) the ground-up malted barley is pumped in. The enzymes in the barley then convert the corn starch into sugars, and the mix runs into the top level of pipes, the temperature steadily dropping to 23°C (73ºF), at which point yeast can be added.

We're now underneath the enormous triangular steel legs of the fermenters, which Maemura tells me blithely take 24 hours to fill. After three to four days, the wash has reached 10-10.5% ABV and is ready to be distilled.

It has taken me years to get my head around grain distilleries. Again, it's to do with their size. When you are in a still house of a malt distillery you can work out what happens in the pots. In goes the mash, it's boiled, vapour rises, then it's turned back into liquid that's stronger. Then repeat, but this time select the flavours you want.

Grain distilleries on the other hand use column stills and they are enormous, many storeys high and often linked in complex fashions making it impossible to follow what is happening. The blind men trying to work out what an elephant was like had it easy compared to this.

It can be explained by diagram or, better still, models, but these have

A Shinto shrine sits outside Chita's door.

none of the physicality of a malt distillery, where the sight and smell of things happening gives you a notion of how things progress. At a grain distillery you simply accept that there's cooking and injection and cooling and fermentation and distillation, because it happens out of sight.

Most grain plants I've been to are indoors, meaning that you can't work out how big the columns are. You'll be shown a room with a massive cladded trunk of a thing and told that this is only one small piece of it. The action takes place many storeys above. And you can't see that because a) it's all happening inside the column and b) distillers in my experience are somewhat leery at letting clumsy writers anywhere near heights. Especially after lunch.

Chita, though, is outdoors and Maemura has no problem with letting us get up close and personal with the business end of distillation. We climb onto a walkway linking the offices with the distillery, up another level, and another, and we're beside the condensers. From here, those silos now seem small. There's the smell of the sea and the dry dock opposite, mingling with the whiff of sweet cereal. Now, there's a sense of Chita's spirit. Take and I walk around, up ladders, looking at the arcing copper pipes of the four condensers, which can be linked in a variety of ways.

That's important to Chita's style, or styles. Remember, the major distillers in Japan do not trade stock. Also, bear in mind that high-strength

A maze of pipework can make a visit to a grain distillery confusing.

The enormous grain silos and fermenters at Chita.

grain whisky does have character. In Scotland, where trading is normal practice, that means blenders can choose between grains from different distilleries. Here it means – you guessed it – the distillery making more than one style: clean type, heavy type and, in the middle, one of those terms that when translated seems so *kawaii*: 'tasty type'.

'We have to make several different types of grain for the varieties of blended whisky, because every one of our blends has Chita grain,' says Maemura. 'In the 1990s, we made the decision that quality was the most important thing, so we started research and development. Sales weren't that good, but we had enough time for research! We began the development of the different types from this point, initially with light and heavy.'

This means maximizing the influence of each of the columns. The heavy type is made with the first two columns (the analyzer and rectifier); medium type uses the analyzer, an extraction column, then the rectifier; while the clean type uses all four, with the last column being used to remove very specific flavours.

It sounds complicated – and to some extent it is – but the principle is simple. The alcoholic wash that is being distilled contains a huge number of flavour compounds, each of which has a different boiling point. By distilling in a tall column, that block of flavours is stretched out. Each column that is added stretches it even further so that only the lightest flavours end up being condensed. In simple terms, the more columns, the lighter the spirit.

The rectifying column next to me is divided into chambers. Inside, the vapour is rising, chamber by chamber. At each one, the heavier flavours

will slump back, refluxing back into liquid, while the lighter ones continue their journey upwards.

The result of making three styles is extra layers of complexity for the blends. Grain isn't a diluting agent in a blend, but an active participant in terms of flavour and texture while also being the ameliorator between often awkward single malts. Having good-quality grain, or rather good-quality grains, is of crucial importance in blending.

We walk back to do a tasting in something you don't expect to see at a grain distillery, a presentation room. It points to a fundamental change in the way Chita is being talked about, and now sold. Chita is now a brand, 'The Chita' in fact, and as a result, bartenders and trade are coming to the distillery to be shown how it is made.

It shows an acceptance on the part of Suntory that there is nothing to be embarrassed about here. Chita may be a vast web of pipes and vessels, towers and silos, but this is also a place where a vital part of the firm's whisky's vision is created – and creation is the correct term. It might be impossible to make small-scale experiments here – hence the need for the grain still at Hakushu (see page 68) – but Chita operates its own form of flexibility.

Outside the distillery, a section from one of the columns lies between some trees like a piece of an alien spacecraft, its exquisite verdigris the same shade as the leaves of the tree, soft and hard, industry and nature linked. The ugly child is no longer being hidden from sight. Instead people can see it is in fact beautiful and that the people working here have as much dedication to their craft as any other whisky-maker.

Chita's three new-makes may be delicate in nature but are distinctly different, particularly in texture. The Light expression has gentle corn, grapefruit zest, a light floral edge and a sugary-smooth palate. The Medium on the other hand has more corn notes: roasted corn cobs in fact, along with a green-banana element. There's also more weight in the middle of the mouth. The Heavy mixes rapeseed oil with some licorice sweetness on the nose and a fat, chewy, and almost malty palate.

After ten years in American oak, the Medium has picked up hot buttered popcorn, caramel and maple syrup with a mace-like palate, while the Heavy at the same age has retained its fatness but added more fruit, ripe banana, coffee bean and roasted pepper.

Some of the components for The Chita are finished in red-wine casks which add a subtle dry spice, plum and raspberry to its crème brûlée-like nose. A seven-year-old in new Spanish oak is, amazingly, not wood-dominated. Instead a new cream toffee and mineral element is brought out, along with resin and clove. Chita, it would appear, is a highly flexible member of the blender's armoury.

The Chita (43% ABV) has a soft aroma of cassia, crème caramel and cashew backed with cream toffee, delicate coconut and macadamia. The palate is akin to banana flambée, plantain chips and those dry spices. Soft and yielding in texture, it becomes sweeter with water or soda.

Chita produces more than one style of grain whisky.

【Configuration whisky】
CHITA Clean

【Configuration whisky】
CHITA Heavy

【Configuration whisky】
CHITA Wine Cask

Suntory Whisky' CHITA'

THE CHITA SUNTORY WHISKY

Chita to Nagoya

The train shakes us back into Nagoya's sleekness and the shopping mall that envelops the station. Outside is a slightly incongruous giant statue of a woman with her legs astride. Children lie underneath looking up her skirts. There are a few furtive glances from some men on their way home. Next to this, but unconnected, is a small standing bar, all blond wood and clean lines, dedicated to one brand, The Chita.

We enter, averting our eyes from the statue. This being Japan, the first thing that you are given is a hot towel, then a small bowl of clam broth, based on an umami-rich, unctuous *dashi* closely followed by a Highball (made with The Chita, of course). It's a calming moment.

I can imagine myself as a harassed office worker coming in here and the towel/broth/Highball being a punctuation mark in my hectic day, a moment to exhale. 'Wine has history and manners,' says Maemura. 'We should have the same with Japanese whisky: the water, the ice, the pairings.

'The broth,' he continues, 'is light, to show the delicacy of Chita, but also its texture. It prepares the palate.' The bartender/chef busies himself with other bites. There's a short Highball menu – you can choose from garnishes of *sudachi* (a citrus fruit), *sakura* (cherry blossom), sour plum and *sanshō* pepper, or there's a '24-hour *mizuwari*'.

Sudachi is one of my favourite Japanese citrus fruits (out of the country's seemingly endless variety) so that has to be tried, but a 24-hour *mizuwari*? The bartender explains: it's The Chita mixed 1:3 with water and left in a container for 24 hours, then served chilled. Why leave a simple whisky and water for a day, other than to save you a tiny bit of time making one? He pours me a 24-hour one then makes me one fresh, to the same ratio. The difference is marked. The 24-hour is thicker, more textured. 'It has umami?' I say. Maemura nods and smiles.

Blenders use different analogies for the role of grain – part of an orchestra, pasta (the malt is the sauce), and so on. Maybe, though, it's *dashi*, the almost invisible base broth, that adds feel as much as flavour, the element in a dish which you miss to begin with but

which you slowly begin to look for. The *dashi* after all is how that dish can succeed or fail.

We are so surface-oriented in the West, so keen to applaud the bold and the brash, the ornately decorative, and forget what lies beneath, what provides them with the platform. We praise the loud and and forget the intriguing subtle whispers of truth.

'People are now looking for new whiskies, not just malts,' says Maemura. 'We have new drinkers coming into whisky from *shōchū* and beer. We have to give them a whisky, and a serve, which they will like.' It makes sense. If they have been used to more gentle flavours (the beer he's talking about is Japan's standard light lager and not its growing 'craft' beers) then don't scare them with peat smoke. That said, The Chita is not wimpy. It's not whisky that's had character stripped out. The mistakes of the 1990s are not being repeated.

There is another, more prosaic, commercial reason. At a time when there is a squeeze on stock of malts, there is conversely plenty of mature grain. If you are making more than one style at a distillery then why not blend them and produce a characterful new whisky which can be sold in volume. Grain – and it's not just The Chita, but the pioneering work done by Nikka's Coffey Malt and Grain, and Gotemba's range – is widening the remit of what whisky is. Grain isn't the future, but it is part of one.

I think back to the days of News and Q1000 and think how far we have come by starting to talk about flavour. Don't change the whisky. Change the occasion, the serve and the mindset.

Nagoya to Kyoto

The Highballs are just a starter, though. OK, we have a train to catch, but this is Japan; there's always time for food. This is also Nagoya, and Nagoya has its own very distinct specialities, all of which I am about to try at once. There is miso *katsu* (pork cutlet and miso), there is sticky *teppazake* (buffalo wings), there are 'slippery beef organs' and dried, roasted red mullet roe and salmon belly, chicken sashimi with wasabi, and most excting of all, eel in Nagoya's miso. No-one had told me about Nagoya's miso. If they had I'd have found a reason to come here every trip. It's dark red, intense, powerful, addictive. Japanese food, subtle? Not here.

At home, I'm used to being able to buy two kinds of miso if I'm lucky. Here every region, prefecture, sometimes village, has its own take. It's daft to think that Nagoya wouldn't have its own. Who would have thought it was this … amazing, though?

We drift back towards the station. My love of eel has already been declared and it's eel season. That means there is now suddenly time to slip into a station restaurant (not something I'd do in the UK, but here? Point me to the terminus, please). The speciality here is *unagi hitsumabushi* (eel three ways). You start by eating a little of the pot of eel and rice. Then you add

the seasoning (spices, pickles and so on), and eat a bit more. Then you add hot tea and stir it in. Three different flavours, three textures, three sensations. It's absurdly simple, absurdly delicious. Like so much of Japanese cuisine, art even, it comes from poverty. If you have little, then you maximize what is there.

As that great commentator on Japan, Donald Richie, says in *A Donald Richie Reader*, '[Japan has] an attitude to nature which was based on penury. If you don't have furniture you pay a lot of attention to empty space. And if you have only mud, then you pay a lot of attention to pottery. This attitude based on want leads to all sorts of interesting things, like *wabi* and so forth.'

There's just time to grab some miso from a convenience store – I am already regretting passing on the Lake Suwa soba, and this isn't going to elude me – and jump on the train to Kyoto.

There are strands flying around: seasons, quietness, regionality, poverty, space, texture, boldness/subtlety, *shibui*, flavour and texture, the role of nature. Still to be tested is whether this idea of whisky-making being allied to traditional craft is real. The next few days will show whether that is fantasy or not.

A novel way to display a menu.

Texture is as important as flavour in Japanese cuisine.

UMAMI

I'm old enough to remember when saying 'umami' would elicit blank looks. 'U-what?' people would say, and then laugh. Now pretty much everyone knows about it. It was described to me by a Californian winemaker as being the 'oo-mammy' sense of deliciousness.

The term was first used by a chemist, Kikunae Ikeda, in 1908. He had noticed a similar quality in various foods, particularly *dashi*. Analysing them, he discovered it came from the amino acid glutamate, and/or the nucleotides inosinate and guanylate, alongside minerals such as sodium and potassium. When it was present in foods they had the oo-mammy quality.

It is there in *kombu* (the base for *dashi*), asparagus, shiitake mushrooms, slow-cooked meat, tomatoes and in fermented goods like soy, fish sauce and cheese. Ikeda went on to create MSG, but we'll pass on that.

Since then, it has been shown that there are receptors on the tongue which are triggered by umami. It is therefore a taste.

Is it there in whisky? Technically no, but there are fatty acids in whiskies – especially non chill-filtered ones – which have a similar rounded quality. Texture is important when tasting whisky – the feel, the way the whisky moves, coating the tongue, filling the mouth.

That delivery matters as it adds to the whisky's complexity and balance. Jota Tanaka speaks of his three styles of grain whisky as being 'the three umami brothers'. The idea of grain whisky as *dashi* is linked to this. In Japan, texture plays a vital role in food and drink.

It's something I always look for, but by now it is becoming obsessive. It's Take's fault. Plate by plate, bowl by bowl, he's adding to my knowledge and changing the way I approach tasting. As Donald Richie writes in *A Taste of Japan* (1993), 'Textures ought to be opposite and complementary: hard/soft; crisp/mealy; resilient/slippery.' If that is the way you are brought up to think about food in Japan, then it is only logical to think that it's an element of significance to its whisky-makers. They're not just thinking of what it smells and 'tastes' like, but how it feels.

Yamazaki

山崎蒸溜所

Kyoto

An early enough start at the Granvia Hotel in Kyoto station. My head is still full of thoughts of Nagoya miso, the possibilities of grain whisky, and where the next eel will be coming from. I rendezvous with Take, having missed breakfast (again), which could account for miso and eel being uppermost in my mind this morning.

Later will be Yamazaki, but first we walk down a long corridor in Kyoto where the light is diffused through huge sheets of textured and patterned *washi* paper. It's half-gallery, half-atelier. We sit as giant sheets of *washi* paper (2.7 x 2.1 metres/8 feet 10 inches x 6 feet 10 inches) are pulled out like canvases, each one more remarkable than the last: silvered paper that changes texture and colour, depending on how the light strikes it; one that shows drops of rain on one side, transformed into a multicoloured waterfall when lit from the back; others with holes. Constellations and jet streams, fields of energy, the flow of the seasons. Abstracted reality. All are the work of Eriko Horiki.

Washi is made from mulberry pulp and water, formed into shape on giant screens, the patterns created by placing mulberry bark, silk, or cotton thread on the surface. The swirls of colour emerge after buckets of dyed fibres are tipped onto the screen, the holes made by Horiki splashing the surface of the forming paper with water.

A piece can take five months to complete and will comprise between three and seven layers, some patterned, some coloured, each less than 1mm ($\frac{1}{400}$ inch) thick. The cumulative effect is dazzling, baffling. Take and I look at each other, grin, shake our heads, and mouth, 'How is this possible?'

Calm and energy in paper and gravel.

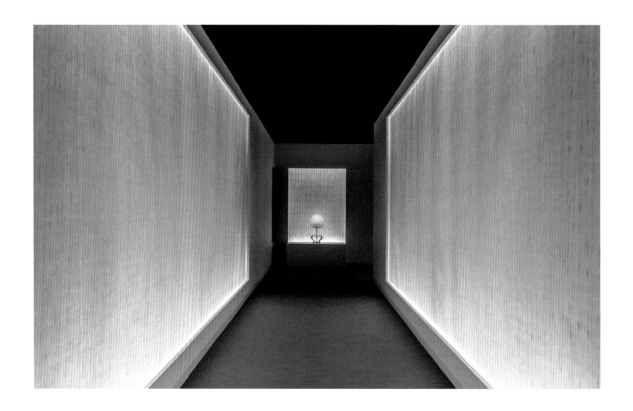

WASHI

Paper is important. It speaks of a shift from oral to written culture. It records, it carries messages, it wraps, enfolds and encapsulates. Papermaking has taken place in Japan for 1,500 years and *washi* sits at the apex of the craft. Until recently though, *washi* was not considered to be an architectural medium. There again, no-one ever told Eriko Horiki this. Her pieces now hang in luxury hotels and upmarket shopping malls. A massive example is in the prime minister's residence, another in a chapel. The labels for Suntory's top whiskies use her paper, albeit on a smaller scale.

Dressed elegantly in black and white, she is serene, but not aloof. Every statement is accompanied by a smile or laugh.

Perhaps unsurprisingly I presumed that her work must be the culmination of years of training, art school, maybe a family background in paper craft, but no. She grins. 'I have no art training. I worked in a bank, then in the accounts department of a paper factory. One day my colleagues were going to a *washi* workshop in Imadate, Fukui Prefecture, so I went along.

'It was winter and very cold. The factory was freezing and all the craftspeople were constantly putting their hands in this freezing water, but they remained enthusiastic about their craft, even in these conditions. Their hands were going purple with cold!

'I was amazed that not only had *washi* culture been here for so long, but saddened when they told me that smaller traditional factories were closing and mechanized factories were taking over. I wanted to try and save the culture.'

She was 24. It's a significant leap from that altruistic impulse to this.

'I had no training, but I had a vision.' She pauses. 'I began to study Japanese craft and why and how people made things. I figured out that this philosophy is in our DNA. Humans have a mind to create. It is not learned; it is in the heart. It is why culture happened.'

The major issue facing *washi* producers was not only that machine-made paper was cheaper, but that its old uses were disappearing. Originally produced for artists, in more recent times it has been used primarily to wrap gifts – the better the gift, the better quality and purer the paper used. In order to save the workshop she had to find a new use for *washi*.

She began to commission the workshop to make the huge sheets used in her work. Today, her Kyoto studio makes even larger ones.

The self-taught Eriko Horiki has transformed the possibilities of *washi*.

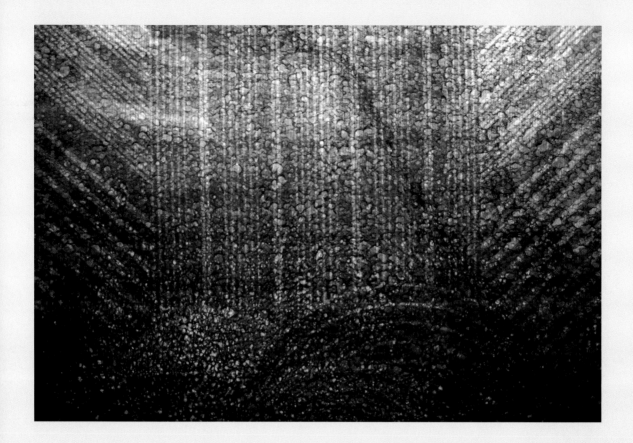

So she preserved the tradition by moving forward?

She nods. 'At school in Japan we are taught that heritage and innovation exist in opposite worlds, but the reason that handcrafts have survived for 1,500 years is because they were innovative. Nothing lasts without innovation.'

In other words, heritage is just the innovation of the past and innovation is the heritage of the future?

She nods again. 'If I had been craft-educated I wouldn't have been able to do what I've done,' she says. 'I came out with these flexible ideas because I am not craft-trained and didn't know what the restrictions were!'

Maybe only an outsider can see what can be done to save a craft by moving it on. All the way through my chat with Horiki, words from my conversations with whisky-makers appear. Subtle, craft, tradition, small details, the need for constant movement and improvement. Shared beliefs.

Before she could start on her vision, she also had to understand paper on a deeper level. 'It has a spiritual side,' Horiki explains. 'In Japanese, paper is called *kami*, which is also our term for "god". We think there is a connection between us and the gods, so making white paper helps us purify our minds and link us to them. That is why we wrap presents in pure white paper. I believe *washi* has purity and stability, and I want to express that balance of subtle strength.'

But she colours it and punches holes in it!

She laughs. 'The craftspeople did try to stop me, but each piece has many layers, and in every one there is one pure white sheet.'

I think of the paper with holes in it and how it now seems almost sacrilegious, and about paper's weakness rather than its strength.

'When they saw the holes in the paper they thought I was insane. They saw it as destroying the paper. In the beginning, I was trying to make perfect paper and when I dropped something on it, it was ruined. Then I thought, "Why not have holes all over?" It's no longer ruined; it has become art.'

The finished pieces are hypnotic in the way they change colour, pattern, even at times apparently shape depending on light. They calm the mind and they flow, showing the strength of the material, but also its fragility. The holes, I think, speak of impermanence, the impossibility of purity and the beauty achieved as a result. The 'flaws' make it perfect.

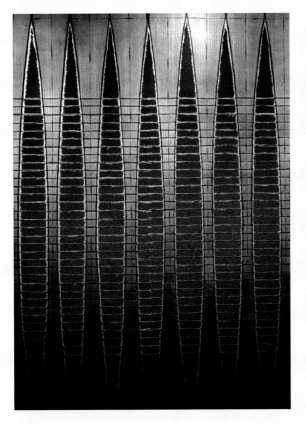

'Each piece has an energy, a meaning, a spirit. It's a narrative or a story. If a client wants something for a building, I think what's beyond the company, what's the spirit, because the paper itself has a spirit.'

Does she sense a shared philosophy with other crafts?

'For me, craft is understanding the inherent tension between tradition and making something to suit today. It's also about respecting nature and life and making something that will be worthwhile for someone.'

Did she have to compromise?

'When I started, I wanted to control it all, but if you want to make something "perfect" then make it with a machine. *Washi* has my feeling, and also something which I cannot handle. Making these pieces is about design and skill, but also chance. The final piece depends a lot on temperature and humidity.

'When we make the coloured patterns, everyone pours their bucket of dyed fibres at the same time, but everyone will have their own timing or force, so only 70 per cent of the original intent is in the finish. Splashing is design, but there is also an element of natural choice – where the water falls, how hard I flick it. The end result is about a willingness to open up to chance, and allowing plans to change as nature impinges itself on the process.'

She smiles again, nods slightly. She's busy; we have a distillery to get to.

The remarkable creations of Eriko Horiki.

Kyoto to Yamazaki

Horiki's parting comments kept running through my skull as we dodged the usual mash-up of school kids, businessmen, tourists and monks at Kyoto Central. If innovation is just tomorrow's heritage, then perhaps chance is what drives the innovation, and that chance forces the makers to improvise, to open themselves to the forces of nature. Any art, any -dō, no matter how apparently rigid and process-driven, has to be willing to accept chance and change.

We get the local semi-rapid service in the direction of Osaka and get off at Yamazaki. As usual, there's only another couple of folk alighting here. I've walked the road to Yamazaki many times. On my first day in Japan, I stepped out of the station, stunned by jetlag, senses already overloaded, carrying whisky-writer Michael Jackson's hefty bag of books. Every time I return, I see myself, younger, walking the same route. These ghosts meet for a second and I wince at the idiocy of some of my questions at the distillery, how I have changed, grown more grey, more bearded. I've walked here in every season, in the dripping heat of summer soundtracked by cicadas' deafening techno; in gentle autumn; in chill winter; and in the expectant vibrancy of spring. Always the same path, but always different, always new.

It was only after a number of visits that someone casually said, pointing at a plain old wooden building next to the station, 'You do know that's Miyoikan, Sen no Rikyu's (see page 157) first teahouse?' He is never far away, and is about to come closer.

You crest the hill, take a left, then a right and there is the old post showing the border between Kyoto and Osaka; beside it is an ancient inn which serves the finest noodles, and a shrine, Sekkidai Myōjin, which commemorates the great battle fought here in 1582, when the samurai Toyotomi Hideyoshi revenged the death of his lord and began his own ascent to power and the unification of Japan. This old road has many tales.

On that first day I knew none of this. I didn't even know what the distillery was like. I suspect I was thinking of something impressive but modest, but just as the road straightens out beside the shrine, Yamazaki's brown brick bulk commands the view and as you walk along the narrow, straight part of the road, between the grey-tiled houses with their *tanuki* (raccoon dog) protectors, avoiding cars and scooters, it continues to rise: bulky, solid, looming.

It is the Japanese distillery that I have visited most frequently. It is – I realize this time, my head filled with yet more theories – where I come to learn and test out those mad new ideas on one of my oldest and dearest teachers, Suntory's chief blender, Shinji Fukuyo.

We have talked process, and blending. We have worked on language, spoken of innovation and at the end of every visit another layer has been revealed – not, I think, because anything has been withheld, but because my knowledge has been allowed to deepen.

It is only by revisiting a place either physically or through tasting that the questions can form. This is the place of another beginning for me: the first day, the first distillery, the first *mizunara* (see page 90), the first use of the term 'transparency', and that sense of newness has never left.

Some distilleries are comforting. You slip back into a familiar world of creaks, quirks and scents yet they always offer up something different as you go deeper into the familiar. Yamazaki, though, is constantly renewing itself, seemingly existing in a continuous, restless present.

The tranquility of Yamazaki's woods.

YAMAZAKI

山崎蒸溜所

It starts with water. Then religion.

No distillery is just a production facility. Every one has a backstory, has been impinged upon by history. Even Chita, that most industrial of plants, has a human face when you get to know it. Yamazaki, though... Yamazaki has depth. Whisky-making is merely the latest event to have taken place on this site. Samurai have fought here, people have prayed and made tea, they have thought and philosophized, they have dreamed and built upon those dreams. Yamazaki is at once the starting point and the hub around which all Japanese whisky still spins.

All of that isn't immediately obvious when you stand at the level crossing at the end of the old road and wait–in my case with a certain degree of trepidation–for the barriers to rise. There are seven tracks to cross and it seems to me there's never quite enough time.

If Hakushu (see page 56) is in a forest, then Yamazaki is part-arboretum where every tree seems to be labelled. Only in the steeply rising hill to the back, filled with bamboo and *hinoki* does some sense of wildness remain.

We walk past the huge multistoreyed former maltings on the left, the swish new visitor centre on the right. A party of school kids are finishing their tour. This isn't an unusual sight in Japan, though I suspect the suggestion of a school trip to the local distillery would cause outrage in Britain. No wonder we have such a messy relationship with alcohol.

Shinji meets us outside the admin building. He has spent time as Suntory's man in Scotland, and managing the firm's distilleries in Japan, before returning to the blending team where he worked under Seiichi Koshimizu, whom he replaced in 2011.

We stand beside two statues, one of Suntory's founder, Shinjiro Torii (1879–1962), the other of his son, Keizo Saji, the man who created the premium whisky category. Beside them is one of the original pair of pot stills Torii installed in 1923. Though now disused, its shape is once again being used here.

But why build here? Torii was Osaka-based; he knew the future market for whisky would be in the major cities, Tokyo, Osaka, Kyoto,

Impressively sized, Yamazaki was Japan's first purpose-built whisky distillery.

Nagoya and so on, so there was a sound economic reason, but there's more. There's the water. The Uji, Katsura and Kizu rivers merge close by, adding a misty humidity deemed good for maturation by Torii. Close by is the Rikyu no Mizu spring, named as one of the top 100 waters in the country (its source has a shrine on top).

Markets and water then, but there's more. We're walking, not towards the distillery but away from it, uphill to a huge red *torii* gate that leads steeply uphill to a cluster of Shinto shrines.

'This area was originally a huge Buddhist temple complex that stretched all the way to where the railway is now,' explains Shinji. 'The temple was established in 764 and extended after the battle of Yamazaki, when Hideoshi sent for Sen no Rikyu to do the tea ceremony.' It was here then that Rikyu began the process of refining the drinking of tea into something which was humble and equalizing, that concentrated the mind on the small details – on craft and detail. It's hard not to see the same impulse remaining at work. The fact that Hideyoshi ordered Rikyu to commit *seppuku* (ritual suicide) in 1591 should maybe be glossed over at this point. No chief blenders have been harmed in such a way.

After westernization, there was a shift from Buddhism to Shinto and many of these old temples changed to shrines. Here among the trees are four of them. 'Shinjiro believed in these gods,' Shinji tells me.

So this was no distillery plot, this was a blessed place, a holy place. Torii the chemist, the toothpaste-maker (one of his first jobs as a chemist), the producer of *yo-shu* (the ersatz Western-style spirits made in the 19th century) was also deeply attached to the resonance of place and spirit.

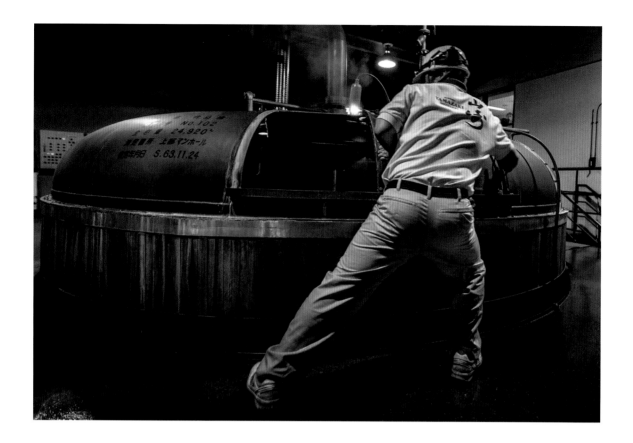

Yamazaki has two mash tuns.

His whisky journey started when he began to be fascinated by wood-aged drinks, be they wine (his first product was Akadama 'port') or whisky. 'At the same time [as he started Yamazaki] there was westernization,' Shinji continues, 'but by the 1920s Japan was entering an economic depression and all of the money being made in whisky was leaving the country into the pockets of Scottish and American distillers. He wanted to keep it in Japan. He was always thinking about his country—and he liked whisky!'

With Masataka Taketsuru (see page 210) by his side as distillery manager/distiller, Torii got to work and in 1924 the first spirit ran. In 1928, the first Japanese blend, Shirofuda (White Label) was launched. Inspired by Scotch, it was not only smoky, but too smoky. It was too heavy, too hefty, too much like hard-core Scotch to appeal to the Japanese consumer. Its lack of success, however, was vital to the creation of an identifiable Japanese style. Failure focused and refined Torii's vision, as well as causing the split between owner and distiller. Now there were two streams of thought.

If you want to mark the moment when Japanese whisky (rather than whisky from Japan) started, it's not the experiments of the 1920s, but the brands that appeared in the 1930s, especially Suntory's new blend, Kakubin, which was launched in 1937.

'The Japanese palate was not used to the European flavours. Red wine was too bitter, whisky was too smoky,' Shinji explains, 'but at the same time you have people wanting to eat and drink better, so [Torii] had to meet a requirement of quality.' Was it really as simple as that? If Japanese whisky was to succeed, Torii realized, it had to appeal to the masses. That was his genius.

The volte-face in terms of style — away from smoke and towards a lighter style — is also the first evidence that Japanese whisky-makers were willing to change their product and techniques to suit the sensibilities of the consumer, an approach that continues here today.

For starters, there are two mash tuns, both full lauter, of different sizes. The smaller (which can hold up to 18 tonnes, depending on the style of whisky being made) was installed in 1989, when the distillery was completely reconfigured in order to produce a different style or styles of single malt.

The year 1989 was when everything changed. It saw the end of the classification system, the rise of Scotch, and as in the days of Shirofuda, a re-examination of what Japanese whisky was, and could be. In Yamazaki — which had been launched as a single malt five years earlier — this meant making a distillery within a distillery, one with a smaller mash tun, wooden washbacks and dedicated (and smaller) stills.

The style changed. The smaller stills produced a fuller, fruitier, estery style. In 2005, a further expansion took place. The style deepened that little bit more.

In general, the malt used is either unpeated or heavily peated, but these two streams can also be blended. The malt varieties used are predominantly from the modern range grown in the UK, but some of the older strain of Golden Promise is also used.

Wooden washbacks are used for flavour purposes.

By having a range of different still shapes, Yamazaki widens the range of flavours it makes.

The wort is, inevitably, clear. 'The milling ratio is very important so we are looking for a bigger husk percentage so as to get a good filter bed,' distillery manager Fujii-san explains. 'We then only cut the top of the bed to get some filtration and run the mashing cycle very slowly.'

Doesn't having more husk mean making less spirit per tonne of barley? Shinji grins. 'It's either the character you get from clear wort, or better yield. We are allowed to create better whisky even if it means higher costs and less efficiency. If it works for quality we'll do it, because ultimately quality will make profit.'

The washbacks are now all wooden because part of the shift to fruity character meant longer fermentations and the need for active lactobacilli (see page 59). 'In general, we run the ferments for three days and use two types of yeast,' says Fujii-san. 'There will always be brewer's yeast used. Research shows distiller's yeast converts sugar quickly, but brewer's adds complexity.'

We're outside the stillhouse. I remember, as I always do, a Yorkshire accent in my ear as Michael Jackson whispered, 'You won't have seen anything like this.'

He was right. Like Hakushu (see page 56), Yamazaki has a collection of stills of different shapes and sizes. There are six pairs in the main stillhouse, two of the pairs being installed in 1989. Two of the wash stills also have worm tubs, while there are a further two new pairs, installed in 2005, in an extension building, the shapes of the wash stills and one of the spirit stills being modelled on the originals from 1923.

The sepulchral warehouses of Yamazaki.

All on the wash side are direct-fired. 'According to research, we believe direct fire makes more complex and strong aromas, and this character is built in the wash stills,' Shinji explains. 'It's not necessary on the spirit side. It's also why the worm tubs [which also promote heaviness] are on the wash side.'

It is this building-in of body that sets the new Yamazaki apart. In distillation, this also involves a deliberate 'misting' of the wash still, in which a fine haze of particulate matter is allowed to rise higher than normal up the still, helping to add weight.

Conversely, the stills are also cleaned after each distillation to allow copper to rejuvenate, adding to the length of conversation. 'We run eight different distillations,' says Fujii-san. 'Then you factor in the option to use different peating levels, barley varieties – and sometimes different yeasts …' The sentence doesn't need to be finished. You get the idea – there are lots of spirits being made here. For example, the whisky from the #5 pair is broad, yet subtly complex with some oiliness, ripe red fruits, and Yamazaki's signature pineapple. The #2 pair, on the other hand, give lighter fruits, more estery notes, melon and a sweeter nature. The newest stills (modelled on the oldest) are perfumed, fruity and estery but with a medium weight.

This complex matrix is then added to in the warehouses. Though large in size, they are long, with casks only four high, replicating the old 'dunnage' style typical of traditional Scottish maturation cellars. I'm enveloped in the aroma of oak and spirit, peering in the crepuscular light at the stencils on each cask, blowing away the cobwebs on some, fingers tracing the 'JO' on the ends of some indicating *mizunara*, or KTB (Kotobukiya) on the sherry butts. In the distance, a small rectangle of green and gold light draws us onwards.

We're walking through a forest of cask types: new and refill American oak barrels; brand-new, ex-bourbon and refill hoggies; new American oak puncheons; new and refill *mizunara* butts; European oak sherry butts and Bordeaux red-wine casks. Those flavour possibilities are now multiplied further.

Not only is Suntory working with Tokyo University on *mizunara*, and building its own casks, but Shinji and his team visit a selection of sherry bodegas and cooperages every year to monitor the production of their bespoke butts. The wine casks come from Bordeaux, where Suntory owns Château Lagrange.

We emerge into sunlight, beside a small pool framed by acers. A tiny waterfall trickles in. You can see the bottom of the pool, the trees seemingly floating in this reversed world. Transparency.

Post-noodles, we go to the blending lab. It's a privilege to be allowed to intrude into this huge space with its tables filled with sample bottles – for blends, malts and experiments. In a side room is a huge library of whiskies from around the world so the team can keep tabs on developments and shifts in style elsewhere.

It's time to taste. We start with the same distillate from 2003 in three different casks. Puncheons give a relaxed, gentle, slightly sweet, custard-accented character with hints of fruit and *tatami* (floor mat made from reeds), while a hoggie adds vanilla overtones to a more overt, ripe baked pineapple, banana and pepper. Ex-bourbon casks have the richest extract, giving honey, juicy fruit, milk chocolate and a gentle hint of coconut backed with a crisper structure – and more acidity.

As more and more samples appear, so the immense variety of options available begins to develop: an opaque, resinous, tannic 1989 from Spanish oak that shows licorice, coffee and scented peppers; a refill Amerian oak from 1992 has a ripe (umami-like) and slightly citric edge, some rhubarb, ginger and classic Yamazaki light fresh fruits. And so it continues: vanilla, *sanshō*, incense, *onsen*, tobacco leaf, dried peels, sour plums, yet all somehow identifiably Yamazaki – that fruit, the pineapple, the light acidity.

All of these could go into blends, or the single-malt range, each expression of which is a different blend of Yamazaki's many characters. The Distiller's Select NAS, for example, is made up of different components to the 12- or the 18-year-old. All are Yamazaki, but all are different.

For all the talk of research, it is clear that location somehow remains a potent element. 'Summer is so hot here that we need bigger casks for maturation, so you concentrate the spirit and not the wood,' Shinji explains. 'You also get more extract here and at Ohmi [Suntory's main warehousing site close to Kobe] while you get a completely different result from the same whisky in the same cask type at Hakushu. Also, Yamazaki's microclimate means there's higher humidity here – and its warehouses haven't such high roofs so it is different.'

Nothing is left to chance, but for all the scientific investigations and secrets (which I cannot divulge) there is a very human sensibility at work

山崎蒸溜所

here. Nothing could be further from technological whisky-making. This is whisky-making as an alliance of art and knowledge, with the former being the dominant element.

'We are artisans,' Shinji once told me. 'Artists aim to create something new, they are creators. We artisans are responsible for creation, but also to sustain the quality in our products. We have a promise to keep.'

I can understand what makes it Yamazaki, but what also makes it Japanese? Shinji's answer starts, as so many responses have done on this trip, not with whisky, but food. 'In New York you can eat Italian food made by Italians, or Indian food in Britain made by Indians. In Japan, you will eat Italian food made by the Japanese – and look how our curry is different! Our culture is different and we make things our own. It's often the most subtle of things. Also, as a culture we pursue everything to try and make it better and better – though I admit that sometimes the purpose is lost!'

Time to try out a theory. This is whisky-*dō*?

'Yes, but-*dō* isn't just "way", but "the art of" and that means taking many elements into consideration. We care about freshness, and the taste of the thing itself. It's why we focus on quality materials and seasons in *kaiseki*, in sushi, in bartending. It's the same focus. Whisky doesn't mean it is just about liquid quality; it is about the philosophy.'

Which helps in the creation of this 'transparency'?

'We are very good at precise work, and our attitude to whisky-making pays attention to these precise points, so we want to extract wort that's very clear, we want clear flavours from ferment. We want to make a whisky that is pure, with a complex aroma, but with no "noise". It's subtle.

'From my point of view, Japan makes a subtle and sophisticated spirit: soft and clean, made with soft water and deep maturation, with more extract than in the cooler temperatures of Scotland.'

What is Yamazaki then? Less a laboratory and more a living web of artistic and philosophical possibilities living in an eternal present.

TASTING NOTES

A multiplicity of styles is made at Yamazaki.

Like Hakushu, Yamazaki offers an equally inspiring – or baffling – array of possibilities from its approach to distillation. A tasting of some of the different oak types used gives a small indication of the options open to its whisky-makers.

A 2003 in a new oak puncheon is fragrant, with custard, *tatami* and a fresh-fruit palate, while a sample from the same vintage but aged in a American oak hogshead takes things into vanilla, along with the distillery's signature pineapple. The palate brings out stone fruits; an ex-bourbon cask from the same year is more crisp structurally with more milk chocolate, coconut on the nose, but added acidity on the palate.

Ex-sherry oak then stirs in darker and deeper flavours and more structure. A single cask from 1989 is scented with coffee bean, dried gorse flowers, black pepper and resin and desirable grip and astringency, while one from 1994 shows chicory, molasses and balsamic elements. *Mizunara* is an important element in the Yamazaki profile, and an example from 1984 is exemplary in its heady exotic intensity – all old houses and temples, incense, snuff, allspice, long pepper and stone fruits. Amazing, certainly, but the biggest curveball comes with a 23-year-old sample of heavy peated distillate from a refill cask. The smoke has gone, leaving behind a heady swirl of tropical fruits – mango, guava, papaya – and waxiness.

Of the bottled product, the relatively new **Yamazaki Distiller's Reserve** (43% ABV) has a typically heightened, scented, aroma of stewing berries, fruit salad and a hint of smoke. The palate is soft, with the heavyweight element only showing its hand at the very end. This mix of the fragrant and deep is picked up in the **12-year-old** (43% ABV) which also has a dried *tatami*-like aroma, pineapple and a succulent gathering of its forces in the centre of the tongue.

The **18-year-old** (43% ABV) seems to use heavier components plus ex-sherry and *mizunara*. There's some incense, raisin and tamarind in its heavily fragrant depths. The rarely seen **25-year-old** (43% ABV), continues this sherried track but adds more fig, date, balsamic/soy notes and a thick, slightly bitter layering. Obsessives might try to seek out **Yamazaki Sherry Cask** (48% ABV), of which the latest release was in 2016. This has roasted tea, scented wood, new brogues, before finishing, surprisingly, with rose petal, strawberry and, yes, pineapple.

Osaka

We all head back to Suntory's swish new bar/restaurant in Osaka, complete with a shop selling high-end furniture made from old staves. In the restaurant, ladies who lunch mingle with young trendies and business people, all sipping on Highballs, whisky cocktails or bottle buys. Things are indeed changing. The vision of Torii, at times like this, seems complete. Whisky as a drink, accepted and enjoyed – with food, on its own, inter-generational, not restricted to age, sex or income.

Things were not always as easy. We adjourn to a basement and Suntory Bar Taru, owned and run by the 87-year-old Koji Wada who has been behind the stick for 55 years. He started his career by pushing a mobile bar with a one-tonne tank of water in its roof around the streets of Kyoto. He'd find a pitch, swing down the sides, climb inside and dispense drinks. He is also the man who, in the 1950s, trained a new generation of Japanese bartenders.

Who taught him? 'I taught myself!' he laughs. He remembers the good old days of whisky. 'Everyone in those [early] days drank Highballs. A few had it with water, but it was all Japanese: Kaku, Torys, Nikka.

Scotch was three times as expensive.' Then came the slump, but he continued to pour his charming old-style drinks – he has a whole book dedicated to drinks inspired by characters in Shakespeare's plays.

'I was invited to Torii-san's house once at New Year in the 1950s,' he says casually.

What was the house like?

'It was modern, it had fireplaces. Unusual for the 1950s.'

And Torii? 'He was a very calm man. He gave me this piece of calligraphy when he came in once.'

It was a lot to ponder when Take and I got back to the Granvia Hotel. Horiki, Yamazaki, talk of subtlety, innovation, seasons, craft, chance, innovation, quality – and then the man who set Japanese bartending going, with his giant grin, still there, still dispensing wisdom.

The next day would be when it all fell into place.

Koji Wada, veteran bar owner.

CRAFT

Eriko Horiki's talk of the almost-death of tradition and its rebirth in a new form seemed to me to have lessons for whisky, especially the belief that the active tradition of the present is rooted in the innovations of the past. Keeping it alive means doing the same. Fail to recognize that and move things forward and you become marginalized. Innovation, as Leonard Cohen put it, is the 'crack in everything. That's how the light gets in.'

Today would test that theory as it was dedicated to another of those traditional crafts: tea-making. Although coffee seems ubiquitous in Japan, no meeting starts without a bowl of tea being placed gently in front of you.

You can't escape it, but you can escape the tea ceremony, which like so many traditions has become, in Donald Richie's words, 'cultural fossilization'. There comes a point when tradition becomes the ailment rather than the life force; it becomes ossified, unable to move, constricted by rules and regulations.

For a tea fanatic, this was going to be a perfect day. I would sit and learn about tea-growing and tea-making. At least it wouldn't involve instructions in the tea ceremony. Years before, I'd been given a very brief introduction into some (well, one) of the skills needed,

the seemingly simple matter of whisking up some *matcha* (powdered tea) into a thick green liquid the colour and consistency of Humbrol Signal Green paint (code 208).

I'd learned whisking from my grandmother, who, though small, generated extraordinary energy and was a demon at it. However, as far as I can recall she didn't have to hold her whisk in a specific fashion: thumb facing you, first two fingers behind, your hand arched like a bird dipping its beak in the water. And she didn't then have to write a letter M with the whisk in the bowl while breaking up any bubbles as they rose.

Even the way of picking up the ladle and pouring the water seems so unnatural that it requires focus. It looks natural and graceful in the hands of a professional, but the only reason you notice that fact is because these simple tasks have been made conscious, made difficult. It opens the mind to the mundane. That, I suppose, is the point.

Anyway, none of that today. I'd just be asking questions, and drinking tea – and in Uji, whose teas are the Domaine de la Romanée-Conti of Japan.

Craft is about repetition, but also change.

TEA

Although tea bushes were first brought to Japan in the ninth century, it was when the Zen priest Eisai (founder of the Rinzai School) returned from China in 1191 that cultivation started properly. One of the sites where Eisai's seeds were planted was Uji, 17km (10½ miles) to the south of Kyoto. While our tea school, family-owned Fukujuen Ujicha Kobo, isn't quite that old, it has been in operation since 1790.

We go through the rather chi-chi (or cha-cha?) shop and upstairs into a functional space. In one room, a group of visitors (an office department on a day out, by the look of it) is grinding leaves into powder. That's OK; just no whisking, please.

'Please come through,' says the young guide, Shinki Yamashita. 'We'll be working in here.' The room is filled with the smell of tea leaves, fresh, bright, taking me straight back to Hakushu. Hang on: 'working'? There are no mills. Instead there's a series of tables.

No whisking, or grinding either; we're being instructed in the art of *temomi* (hand-rolling). Virtually all tea in Japan these days is mechanically processed. This hands-on approach, the oldest tradition, is rare.

There's that recurring theme again. This idea of Japan as an almost sacred repository of traditional crafts is untrue. They exist, but precariously.

'And it's hard,' he adds. Is that a slightly evil grin? 'You could use technology to make it quicker. We think that this gives the best control over flavour.'

Temomi involves eight separate processes. We stand around the table (*hoiro*). There's little time for note-taking but Take manages to grab the odd second or two for snapping. There's a dark-green mass of single leaves in front of us.

'It's an eight-hour process,' he continues. We look at each other, slightly worried. We have dinner planned, after all. 'We'd better get started. There are 3kg (6lbs 10oz) here. At the end of our work we will have 500g [1lb 1½oz] – if you do it properly.'

The *hoiro* is covered with what looks like the knack-ered, stained sail of an old ship, but is in fact ten layers of paper (the *jotan*). It's also warm to the touch. 'There's heat underneath so that the water will evaporate when we're working. It's usually 100°C [212°F]. We make it less for you.' He smiles. 'And we won't ask for the whole eight hours.' The leaves have already been steamed, sifted, and and allowed to cool.

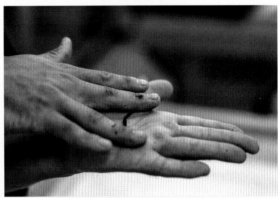

We get to work. Grind the leaves, lift them and rub them between your hands. 'No. Harder. Push them.' A new move. Keep them on the *jotan*. Gather a lump, press with the heel of your hand and squeeze, slowly rolling the leaves. It's like kneading dough, but longer, more rigorous. My back starts to ache, bending over, the *jotan* slowly becoming stained green, as are my hands. 'You have to work fast!' We pick up the pace. 'Squeeze it, press it. This evens out the moisture content, gives even drying.' Each squeeze is helping to break down the leaf's cell walls; the tea is starting to oxidize, its more complex flavours beginning to form.

It's hot, sweaty. I'm reminded of watching sake being made where the brewers, stripped to the waist, would haul the steamed rice and *koji* around the table-tops with bold caresses. Like tea-making, much relies on an understanding of climate and humidity. Where else have I heard that recently? 'We'll know by touch how much water is in the leaves and how best to process and roll.' Tea is a vintage product. Conditions change each year.

Initially, I took Yamashita for a tour guide, but when Take takes over for me, I ask him about the training. 'It takes 15 years to master. My grandfather taught me.' His grandfather? 'Yes, he is a master. In fact, he

is above the other 11 masters.' I can see his influence, though Yamashita is an engaging tutor, he's serious about us doing it properly. This tea is expensive and if you want to know how to make it, there can be no half-hearted attempts.

Another move. Now cupping the leaves between your hands, then rolling and pressing them gently between your palms. Then reverse, repeat, reverse, repeat. 'Find the rhythm. Good. Keep the pressure on. See how they're drier?' And on it goes.

A new move. A board is brought out, sitting at a 45-degree angle to the *jotan*. The bundle is smaller now. Drag and press, more gently now, drag and press. Keep going.

Then another one. Take the bundle. Place your hands on top, fingers splayed. Press down, and make a cut by bringing your wrists together, your fingers splayed out like a bird's wing. Bring the two bundles together, shift the mass 90 degrees, then repeat...and repeat. This last one slowly aligns the leaves. They're beginning to spiral, become more needle-like. He picks

At Fukujuen Ujicha Kobo, making the finest Uji tea is a hands-on process.

one up. 'Not bad.' He picks up another. 'Keep going.' And grins.

'What do you think of when you are working?' I ask. He looks at me.

'I am Zen.' It is the maxim 'When I eat I eat, when I sleep I sleep'. It is being wholly involved in the now. It's *ichi-go ichi-e*, the physical and the meditative.

The final move. Now, we rub the leaves gently again between our hands, soft but firm to get the final spin, then spread them out for a final dry. 'Not bad at all. The best we've had so far this year.' I didn't ask how many have been before.

Perhaps he's being nice, but there again I'm not sure if you'd be polite to idiots who have just ruined high-grade Uji. We'll take the praise. 'You want to do more? We will do this 24 hours a day. There's no sleep in April and May!' We demur. That dinner, you see.

He takes a spoonful of 'our' dried tea and makes a pot, the water at 60°C (140°F). 'If it's too hot, you get bitterness.' It has such umami, such bright greenness, this thick, vegetal, sweet liquid. The first cup is almost *dashi*-like. The second cup – as always – is where the heart of the tea is revealed, layered, fresher now, but also deeper. We raise our tea bowls in a toast.

Where would a tea like this be sold? I ask. 'Many places. Some for the emperor.' (By the end of the evening, this becomes, 'We made the emperor's tea').

'We are looking to export now. Tea-drinking is less popular.' I think of Japan's endless coffee shops, storey-high images of grim-looking Tommy Lee Jones, the face of Boss Coffee, the (hot) cans in vending machines (including the decaffeinated espresso called Deepresso), the cold-drip hipsters creating a new ceremony. That bowl of tea in meetings is no more than ceremony. Tea is becoming worryingly old-fashioned.

A precise series of moves is required.

SEN NO RIKYU

Zen monk Sen no Rikyu (1522–91) can be seen as not only the founder of the tea ceremony, but the initiator of a new approach to craft in Japan. Prior to his innovations there had been a formal Chinese tea ceremony, but he was troubled by its ostentation and how it distracted from the real business: the tea. In the service of Hideyoshi, he stripped everything back to basics to create *wabi-cha*, 'rustic tea' (*wabi* meaning 'simplicity', 'unadorned').

The tea was taken in a small room with a low door that forced all, no matter what rank, to bow on entering. It had minimal decoration, and the teacups were rustic, irregularly shaped. Kazukō Okakura in his *Book of Tea* (1906) described how 'the ceremony [was] intended to inculcate humility, the light subdued, the colours of the clothes unobtrusive, the mellowness of age over all'.

Rikyu is the starting point for the Japanese respect for simplicity, detail, the quality of ingredients. Out of his developments came a new approach to ceramics, lacquerware, metalwork, decoration, tatami, architecture and *kaiseki*.

He said, 'Only by experiencing the arts with one's own body does one understand their true meaning...they are the true gateway to the country's culture.' They can be expressed in something as simple as making a bowl of tea.

There's a lesson for whisky in here. Not just in the calm ritual of a serve, but the way in which you appreciate the spirit: that moment of calm as something made from the humblest of ingredients hits the tongue and floods the senses with flavour and memory. It is also a warning that by relying too heavily on the ritual you restrict enjoyment, and by revering the past you forget the present. Whisky isn't just the fine sip of single malt, it is also the fun of the cocktail or Highball.

Finally, 'our' tea is poured.

CERAMICS

Clutching bags of our tea we go back outside. 'Let's go over to that house opposite,' says Take. 'I've photographed this guy before. He's amazing, a master.' I'm slightly unclear what he might be a master of, and there's little evidence from the exterior, but by now I trust Take implicitly. Inside is a showroom of beautiful teaware (the same cups and bowls we had used) and other ceramics, some made in a clay that seems to be sprinkled with galaxies. The next second a young-looking chap appears from behind a curtain. 'Hello,' he says, bowing and offering a business card, 'My name is Yusuke Matsubayashi. Welcome to Asahiyaki.'

I study the card not just because it is polite but to catch the spelling of his name. Underneath is printed, '15th generation'. I had wanted to include ceramics in my attempts to get to grips with traditional craft, but it had proved hard. Now Take had delivered a man whose family had been involved since the 16th century.

I blurt out something stupid like, 'Four hundred years? That's a long time.'

'But the tea culture is older than that.' He smiles. 'It is because there was that culture around this area that we began to specialize in *chawan* [teaware].' I know that the soil and climate here has an impact on the character of the tea, but what effect does it have on pottery? We walk over to the display and the galaxy bowl I'd admired earlier.

'That's Uji soil,' he says. 'We get this sparkled effect. The tea tastes of the soil, the soil affects the design. Tea came from China, pottery came from Korea. In both cases, Uji soils were considered the best. But while the climate, the soil and the water all have an influence, the sensibility of the people is of equal importance. Would you like to see the kiln?' Hold me back, I'm tempted to say.

The workshop behind is huge. The kiln too. From the front it has the look of a frowning samurai warrior and ripples in steps back into the distance. How do you control something of this size?

'It's like a shrine. When we fire, we always pray to the god of the fire because while we control firing, I can't control everything! But if I was able to, it wouldn't be interesting. There is always something beyond which we have never seen. I can control up to' – he gestures – 'point X, then all the other elements come into play.'

It gets deeper still when he says he has recently returned from a trip to Britain to see the kiln that his ancestor had made for Bernard Leach. Hong Kong-born Leach is one of the key figures in 20th-century British craft. A close associate of Soetsu Yanagi (see page 88), he studied and worked in traditional ceramics in Japan from 1911 to 1920, when he returned to St Ives, initially with his friend and fellow potter Shoji Hamada. (Later he went to Dartington.) When the two men's Japanese-style climbing kiln failed to perform properly, Tsurunosuke Matsubayashi, Yusuke's great-great-uncle, arrived and built a new one for him. It was in use until the 1970s.

Yusuke on his visit got it started again. 'I brought soil from Uji with me and mixed it with that of England and made *chawan* and other works.' It's like Japanese whisky's story, but in reverse.

How, then, would you define your approach as being Japanese? 'It's respecting nature. I know Koshimuzu-san [former head blender at Suntory]. He can control distilling, but when the spirit has to go into wood all he can do is pray! It's the same as me and the kiln. I have to respect nature, process and spirit. Maybe Western artists try more to bring out their personality. I try to bring out the potential of the soil, so I respect the soil and fire.'

It mirrors what master Hamada once wrote. 'If a kiln is small I might be able to control it completely, that is to say my own self can become a controller, a master of the kiln. When I work in the large kiln, the power of my self becomes so feeble that it cannot control [it] adequately. It means that for the large kiln the power that is beyond me is necessary. One reason I wanted to have a large kiln is because I want to be a potter ... who works more in grace than his own power.'

What, though, of the future for craft in Japan?

'The culture has been declining since my father died. The question now is how to interest a young generation in craft. Traditionally, we have always thought of only selling domestically, but exporting is becoming more important. It's selling the wares, but also the culture.' He gives me a book in English about 'the new Kyoto crafts movement'. There's so much more to talk over, but it's getting late and we have to get to dinner. My head is spinning again.

Asahiyaki's samurai-looking kiln (above). Yusuke Matsubayashi, 15th-generation master potter (above right).

'What is craft?' asked Bernard Leach once. His answer was that it's 'good work proceeding from the whole heart and head in proper balance … The heart is fed through the senses, not by the fact-finding, busy intellect of the West but by intuition and emotion, responding to innate behests of material.'

Matsubayashi spoke as Hamada spoke, as his ancestors spoke, but with a very aware modern sensibility. Everything that had been said seemed to mirror what Eriko Horiki and all the whisky-makers had talked about: location, innovation, natural process, lack of ego, respect, simplicity and that wonderful element of chance, because this is a living process, all slowly forming like strands of paper fibre.

Later that night, thinking of the 'galaxy' bowl, I flick through Yanagi.

'The thing shines,' he writes, 'not the maker.'

The galaxies that typify Uji clay.

KAISEKI

The day hasn't even finished yet. There is the not-inconsiderable matter of a *kaiseki* meal ahead. I have done *kaiseki* a number of times and never failed to be astonished and bamboozled by the precision, the focus on ingredient, season and presentation; the complexity within its simplicity. I've sipped the sake and gasped as each course is presented. I've also, it has to be said, on occasion wondered when this overly formal experience was going to end.

I try to behave, I try to sit properly and eat in the correct manner, but I know that as a clumsy, large, hairy *gaijin* (foreigner) I will always screw up at some stage. *Kaiseki* therefore becomes a gourmet delight but one filled with anxiety.

This is to prove different. Not just because it is with Shinji Fukuyo at Michelin-two-starred Ryozanpaku. Or rather, not because of being dazzled by the stars, but because the restaurant is owned by Kenichi Hashimoto, who is about as unlike any two-star Michelin chef as you can imagine. He greets us like old friends then takes his position, arms on the counter, the menu in calligraphy displayed above him.

'Beer?' Of course. No matter where you are, what you intend to eat or drink, the first beverage is a beer. In fact there's even a phrase, *toriaizu birru*, which means 'I don't know what I want to drink so I'll have a beer while I'm making up my mind.' Glasses of lager – Suntory All Malts judging by the head – are brought immediately. '*Kampai*.' I take a sip. It's not Suntory All Malts. It might look like beer but it's a –

'Highball!' roars Hashimoto. 'The meal tonight is whisky *kaiseki*. Koshimizu-san and I have created the concept. Why should people always have to drink sake through the meal? Why not whisky?'

This is *kaiseki* all right, but done in a new and boisterous fashion. We're seated on stools at the counter and watch as he starts to work, somehow managing simultaneously to chat and devize and arrange incredibly complex dishes.

As in the best evenings, the conversation switches with dizzying speed from the serious and philosophical to the absurd, and back again. The season slowly reveals itself – eel (of course) makes an appearance. We chat about crafts and seasonality. 'The next course,' says chef Hashimoto. 'will have something different. We can't just drink whisky all night. This is the roots of *kaiseki*.' Some small glass sake cups are passed around. We toast and sip. Hang on –

'Whisky! I got you again!'

And so it goes on. A dazzling variety of courses, each with a whisky in some form: diluted, accented with a garnish, with *dashi*, in a cocktail. The matches work by contrasting or harmonizing. Different temperatures offer counterpoints and accords. It's Shinjiro Torii's vision writ large: whisky becoming intertwined with Japan's most precious form of cuisine.

The conversation is being led by the meal, moving from seasons to texture. 'If our cuisine is based around the textural, then obviously it will influence you when it comes to making whisky,' says Shinji.

'Whisky is also a journey,' says the chef. 'So is *kaiseki*.' He then begins to explain how the meal of which we are now near the end has also been about water. The way it is used: in cooking, in presentation and how it is slowly removed until 'you reach the summit and reset'. Suzuki's talk of cuisine and garnishes zaps back into focus.

The whisky *kaiseki* Hashimoto has created with Koshimizu is deliberately provocative, but it chimes perfectly with all I've heard over the past day. That to survive you have to look deep and be willing to change. That with respect for tradition comes a need

to chafe against restrictive practices. To take on the highly formalized concepts of *kaiseki* in its birthplace is a bold move, but it has to be done both for the cuisine, and for whisky.

The trick is not to fall for the option of change for change's sake. Innovation is often driven by an insatiable, impatient desire for The New; concern over tradition doesn't matter. Just make it new, shiny, exciting. Inevitably, most 'innovations' fail, but that's of little concern because there will be something equally new along in a second. They have no depth, however, because they aren't rooted in anything other than the desire for something different. The past doesn't matter – unless in an ironic and retro fashion.

This mindset seems to contradict craft. After all, that is bedded in tradition, which is about repetition of moves and strategies. It is not spontaneous; it cherishes the past. It's important that your family has been making tea bowls or paper for hundreds of years.

'In a society that follows tradition,' writes Gary Snyder, 'creativity is understood as something that comes about by accident … It takes a powerful impulse for a student-apprentice who has been told … to "always do what was done before" … to turn it in a new way. What

happens then? The old guys in the tradition say, "Ha! You did something new? Good for you!"'

I came into this unclear whether my theory of links between traditional craft and whisky would hold up. All I could do was ask questions and see if there were any connections. Then, today, it fell into place. Whether working with paper, tea, clay, food or whisky the same answers came, the same underlying principles emerged. The primacy of the natural material, simplicity, modesty, attention to detail; patience and striving for improvement, lack of ego allowing the object to shine, being open to chance. A new chapter seems to have been opened.

Michelin-starred chef Hashimoto has devised a whisky *kaiseki* menu.

Osaka

Another member of the cast joins us. I first met Yuki Yamazaki when he was bartending at the Park Hotel. Since then, he's become a global wanderer, and our paths cross in random places: Toronto, London, Paris, Taipei. He's developed his own range of Japanese cocktail bitters, and is to spend the next couple of days with us as interpreter. A last-minute change of plan has given us a quiet first day together. Well, it's meant to be a quiet day. It turns out to be quite the opposite.

The rejigged schedule means the only official visit will be to Sakai Glass in Yodokawa. This is the go-to supplier for most Japanese distillers' top-end offerings and has been singled out by a couple of contacts as having good whisky-related craftspeople to see. It also means getting to Osaka, a city that past experience has shown always throws a few fun curveballs into anyone's well-planned itinerary. It will also be my first visit to a glass factory.

The taxi roams through anonymous backstreets. I'm not entirely sure if we're lost or not. We probably are. Being lost is my default setting when in Japan. My inability to find most places isn't just exacerbated by a lack of understanding of *kanji* (Japanese ideographs), but bars, for example, can be hidden in side streets, in basements and up skyscrapers, which also house 100 other similar establishments. Many evenings have been spent peering at signs in dark alleys, knowing our destination was somewhere close by. Quite often it would be forgotten as another, equally excellent establishment was discovered by chance. One night, unable as usual to find some recommended joint, I asked for directions in a 7-Eleven. Mysteriously there was a newly married couple, she still in her wedding dress, shopping there.

I had a map, but still there was confusion. 'OK,' I said. 'Where are we?' I figured that if we could find that spot I'd be able to find the pesky hostelry.

This, however, was interpreted as an existential question. 'Ahhh, where are we?' said the bride, perhaps already having second thoughts.

'Where are we?' said the shopkeeper, gazing into space. I never found the bar.

Getting lost is good. It takes you out of a comfort zone, off the main route. You meet interesting people when you are away from that straight road – and what of worth was ever made by following the narrow track of convention, eh?

Anyway, that explains why we're slightly late. The sound of breaking glass should have given the place away. We are ushered into a small room where company president Kotaru Sakai begins to tell his family's tale.

Osaka happily marries tradition with modernity.

GLASS

It transpires that the family actually started as rice merchants. 'A family friend had started making glass,' Kotaru Sakai says. 'My grandfather was then asked to join and then, in 1906, he took over the firm.' 'We've had a relationship with Suntory from the start. My grandfather knew Shinjiro Torii.' It was Sakai Glass that made the bottle for Torii's first brand, Akadama 'port', as well as the first Kakubin bottle. 'We're now working for many distillers.' His eyes move to the display cabinet where there are top-end bottles for all the country's whisky producers.

We begin to chat about how things are developing and just as he is starting to describe how the firm has some form of new process, he pauses. 'I think it's probably easier that we show you.'

With that we're on the factory floor. 'We used to hand-blow all the bottles,' he explains, 'but we've been developing a new kind of process which is more automated. Well, it's a bit of both.' In the centre of the room is what looks like a large metal hive punctured by a series of holes that glow a deep yellow-orange. A web of wires and cables festoons everything.

The hive is being attended to by a swarm of constantly moving blue-coated workers. It's hard to keep up. One thrusts a long pole into a hole and grabs a fat gobbet of the molten glass. For a second it's as if he has the sun on the end of this stick. With one quick movement it's spun next to one of his colleagues – surely too close – who watches intently as it flows into a heavy metal mould. He compresses it ,then pulls out the neck. He slams it shut, there's the sound of a jet of air, a bottle forms, and it's lifted out, now clear. It's picked up by tongs, gazed at intently. It has taken 15 seconds. By this time, the next gobbet is on its way.

All around this central point different teams are thrusting, lifting, spinning, dropping, closing, injecting. Clear, and dusky grey, deep red and blue. Filigree traceries spin into the air and crackle and shatter as they cool. A bottle is rejected, tossed into a skip and explodes on touching. It is elemental, hot, intense and a little scary. Everyone's face is lit by the furnace's permanent sunset. All is concentration. I'm bathed in sweat.

A team has moved away from one of the openings. 'We have to empty it, then we'll start again.' An older guy ambles over with a skip to put the glass in, and a pole with an open-topped metal box on the end. He digs into the spent kiln, pulling out oozing bricks. He

Care, precision and speed are all integral
to glass-making.

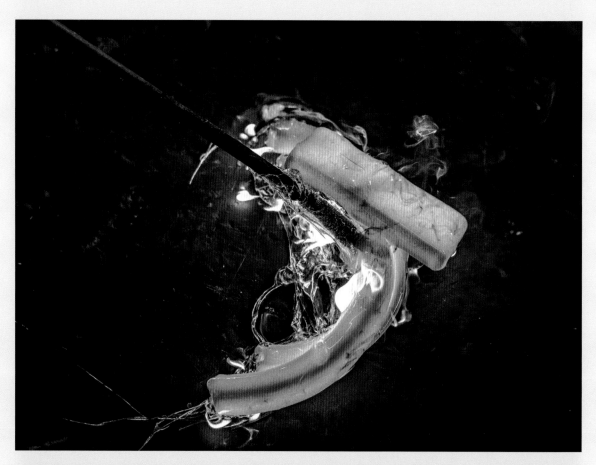

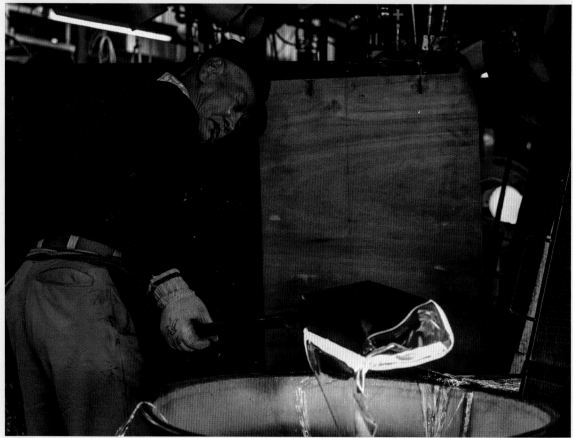

seems to paint streaks of orange in the air. The whole process is transfixing.

'The bottles…' begins Sakai with a smile. Oh yes, the bottles. Those which aren't rejected outright are put onto a glacially slow conveyor belt to cool. 'We'll go to the other end.' It's hard to leave. The workers gaze into the sun, blinded by their work.

It's considerably cooler at the other end of the belt. The bottles, which have now been cooling for for two hours, can be picked up and examined. One is placed on the side. Sakai picks it up. 'It has a flaw.' I look. It seems flawless. 'There.' He points. 'You see now?' There is the tiniest dot. 'The maximum we can allow is 0.5mm.' (about 1/50 inch.) He smiles. 'We are more strict than others.'

We walk past shelves of moulds and old bottles, famous bottles. I pick up an empty bottle of Yamazaki 50-year-old. 'Japanese people like premium quality inside, so the outside has to be premium as well. We have to take care with our craft.'

Make no mistake: this is craft. Downstairs in a small room the designer is sitting, abrading the necks of the stoppers of decanters to get the perfect fit. 'He is remarkable, but craftsmen like him are getting harder to find.' The same refrain. Why then stick with this process? 'We can make 800 bottles a day. Automation will give you more, of course, but being made by one man makes things very special.'

The order books are full. How does he see the craft developing? 'This is a new challenge for me,' he replies. 'Glass is not an Osakan speciality. Japanese glassmakers have relied on machines. Europe is different. There glass is made with style and attitude. I respect the European skills and creativity, because they have history. We haven't got there yet.' He pauses. 'But there are no limits.'

I think back to the first potters comparing their wares to the more highly sophisticated goods from Korea, or Torii and Taketsuru with their first whiskies. Respecting a different tradition, adapting it, making it their own. The same may happen here.

Emptying a furnace at Sakai Glass (opposite). Company president Kotaru Sakai watches intently (above).

Osaka

The management team gather at the entrance to wave us goodbye, or to make sure we get off the premises. We are hungry. Breakfast has been missed. Again. There is considerable discussion. 'I know a place,' says Take. Of course he does. He can scout out the best food in the most unlikely of places and food is what Osaka is about. You might go to Tokyo or Kyoto to dine. In Osaka you come to eat. This is where Japanese soul food rules.

Our choice for lunch, *okonomiyaki*, is a perfect example. What isn't to love about a huge pancake of beaten egg, flour and *dashi* mixed with cabbage and, well, whatever else you fancy (hence the name: *okonomi* means 'what you like'; *yaki* means 'grill') and then dribbled with its own special brown sauce? It's as far from *kaiseki* as you can imagine.

Even here, though, seasons and regional approaches come into play. Spring onions have just come into season,

Take tells us, so now is the best time to go for *negiyaki* where they are the main (indeed sole) other ingredient. A number are devoured.

'I know where we should go,' says Yuki as we sit in the local train back to the city centre. 'Samboa.' Located in a strangely Gothic-looking building, this bar has been operational since 1918, though this location dates from 1947. It has the feel of an old-style saloon: high ceilings, a few tables and chairs, a long bar. There's not a massive range of whiskies. There's no need. At Samboa there's only one thing to drink and it's made in a few seconds.

One tall, cold glass, 60ml (2fl oz) ice-cold Kakubin, one small bottle of soda, lemon twist. No ice. Boom. That's it. The Samboa Highball.

It slips down quickly. So quickly there's a need for a second. I notice that no measures are used – unusual in

the meticulous world of the Japanese bartender. 'Look at the glass,' says the bartender. There's a notch near the base. Well, not that near the base. This is a proper drink. 'That's where the whisky comes up to. See?' Boom. Three more appear. Life is already better. I could stay here all night. I suspect some people do, but we need to check in. 'And then have more food!' adds Take.

You need food to cope with Osaka. This is a city whose residents bludgeon you into submission with friendliness. It's classic second-city syndrome, a condition shared by Glasgow, Birmingham, Boston, Lyon, and so on: places often in the shadow of a more famous neighbour and, as a result, eager to prove themselves by going the extra distance to make you welcome.

You always get sidetracked here. One carefully planned evening of visits to four bars ended up taking in eight as each bartender recommended somewhere else 'on the way', and then joined us. Two of us started out on the crawl. By the end of the evening, 14 of us were across town drinking pre-Prohibition bourbon at Rogin's Tavern.

Home to bars like Augusta, Basara, K, Elixir and Royal Mile, it's also where in my pursuit of the aromas of *mizunara* I first received insights into incense-making. Anything could happen here.

Take and Yamazaki had conversed. 'Real Osaka,' was the conclusion, so we walk to Shinsekai, the once glittering 'New York' district of the city, which now has a seedier reputation – but I kinda liked New York when it was seedy. It is the place to go for *kushikatsu*: battered, panko-coated, deep-fried skewers of meat and vegetables which you dip into thick, dark, sweet sauce. 'Never double-dip!' says Take – as another half-pint mug of draught Highball frosts its way towards me.

Welcome to Osaka!' shout some guys along the counter. 'Don't double-dip!'

Another round of food. There are cabbage leaves to help with digestion.

'Where are you from?' ask the students who have just sat down next to us. 'Scotland? Welcome to Japan! Welcome to Osaka!' They look at my plate. 'Don't double-dip!' Glasses slam together and cold Highball slops on to my jeans.

We dine and drink our way around the city. It's getting late. 'One last bowl!' says Take, spotting a restaurant, then adding his favourite phrase, 'You must

Crab and *okonomiyaki* are on the menu in Osaka (opposite and above).

try this.' We sit at the counter. The chef is standing next to a thick, quietly seething vat of liquid. 'You know *dashi*? Well, this has been simmering for 175 years.' Into this solera are put skewers of daikon, eggs, vegetables and some meat. Late-night, rib-sticking food. We wander home past giant animated crabs and wild sci-fi creatures; puffer fish balloon above our heads. All is neon and noise.

There has always been this side to Japan. For every tea ceremony there has been the floating world of entertainment, for every Noh play there is kabuki, for every hushed whisky bar there is a raucous joint. Whisky lives in both these worlds. It has to. It is there for fun as well as contemplation. No matter its quality or prestige, whisky is, ultimately, functional in the same way as a fine teacup is just a receptacle for tea, or a hand-forged knife is for cutting something. Crafts are functional. Their beauty comes from their purpose and honesty. By revering them as high art we invert them – looking solely at surface and maker, not form, function and purpose.

To understand Japanese whisky, you have to poke under that surface, see what lurks there and work out whether on some level there is a shared philosophy with other crafts. This can manifest itself in a number of ways. Take flavour.

We have a cuisine, now we want a drink to go with it. The cuisine exists because of climate. Summer rains give rice, the meeting of cold and warm ocean currents delivers rich fishing grounds, while a history of poverty has helped to create an aesthetic approach that prizes clarity and precision. This applies to food, or paper, or knife-making, ceramics, and so on. The ingredient isn't hidden, or obscured; rather its qualities are heightened. The drink needs to mirror that. Both are 'transparent', but don't think that means ethereal and wispy; instead it is lucid, unclouded. If Japan had invented whisky and Scotland been inspired to follow its lead, then the Scottish approach would have been different because Scotland's conditions – climate, cuisine, occasion, were not the same. Whisky is cultural and it is natural.

Highballs and *kushikatsu* (opposite left).
Osaka at night can become surreal
(opposite right and above).

HIGHBALL

I've realized that at some point in almost every entry I've mentioned a Highball. Why this apparent obsession? Well, it's a drink that works. Cool, refreshing, just strong enough to know you've had one, but not so strong that you're poleaxed. The drink to start off an evening, or to sip with food.

The Highball is also how Japan's domestic whisky market hauled itself out of an enormous hole. By 2008, an industry that had once sold 225 million bottles a year in Japan alone was selling 50 million. Some distilleries had closed, some were mothballed, the rest were on short-term working; hence the stock shortage today.

As my visit to Zoetrope (see page 94) showed, distillers tried numerous ways to re-energize the market, most of which revolved round making Japanese whisky taste like something else, or nothing at all. All failed. You might have been able to find every whisky under the sun at specialist bars, but in *izakayas* you'd have been lucky to see one glass of whisky being served. Beer yes, *shochu* definitely.

What else could be tried? Suntory Liquors' executive officer Tetsu Mizutani (the firm's 'Mr Whisky') took a gamble. His team reported that there were two whisky hotspots in this desert of rejection. One was the

Samboa group, the other a bar called Rockfish next to Shimbashi station in Tokyo, which was selling a case of Kakubin a day. Both bars were selling Highballs: a double measure of iced whisky, frozen glass, cold bottle of soda, twist if you wanted.

Mizutani signed up 500 *izakayas* across the country to promote Kaku Highballs. Within 18 months 100,000 had joined the campaign. 'We had tried so many other strategies,' he said at the time. 'The biggest reason that whisky wasn't popular was that we had lost the places where people could enjoy whisky. People didn't drink whisky at the end of dinner, or go to that second bar after the meal. They just stayed in one *izakaya* and drank alcohol during the meal. So we decided to try and get them to drink whisky there.' No longer salarymen, but younger drinkers.

The market grew. Every other distiller joined in. Highballs were being served on draught, pre-mixed, and from 'Hiball Towers', Suntory's patented dispensers. They were democratic: the drink of streetside cafés, the train home, or in top-end bars. The answer after all those years of pain was a splash of soda. Why? Because it works. Liquid, occasion, serve. Simple, really.

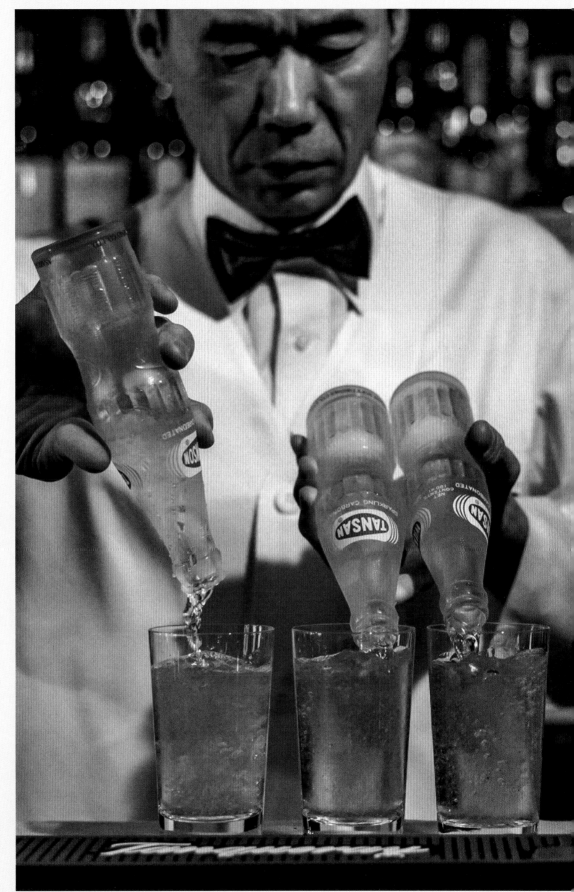

Triple Highball, Samboa style.

BLENDS

In today's world, 'whisky' has become shorthand for 'single malt', despite the fact that the bulk of it is sold as a blend (by which I mean a mixture of malt and grain). It's how Scotch whisky built itself, and Japan followed the same route. It's worth remembering that Japan's first single-malt brand, Yamazaki, was launched in 1984, 60 years after the distillery started producing. Blending gives volume.

Japan's whisky boom was driven by blends, starting with Suntory's Kakubin in 1937. When the same firm's Torys blend launched in 1949, it brought working-class drinkers into the fold–and spawned a 1,500-strong chain of bars and the country's first iconic whisky figure, 'Uncle Tory'. By the 1950s and 1960s the two main firms were looking to premiumize, with Nikka Black, Gold & Gold and Super Nikka; Suntory's Old, Royal (which would become the world's biggest-selling blend in the early 1980s) and, in 1989, Hibiki. Stir in Kirin, Ocean and offerings of often dubious composition from other firms, and you can see how, in those days, 'whisky' meant 'blend'.

The downside was they became ubiquitous. Perhaps single malts are easier to explain. You can see the place, you can even visit it, fix it in the mind.

A blend? It's made … somewhere, by … someone. By the time of the crash, blends were shorthand for cheap, old-style booze. No matter how great many were, in the rush to the bottom to try and sell liquid it was blends that suffered and single malts that eventually rose, untainted, to the top–even though those single malts were themselves blends of different distillates and cask types from one distillery.

The people who make the single malts are the same as those who make the blends, and their dedication to their craft is the same. The blender guides style, maintains the inventory and creates new styles. He or she is a master of flavour. They have to be aware of how the market moves, and shift styles accordingly, as Suntory's chief blender, Shinji Fukuyo, pointed out.

'If we kept the same quality for ten or 15 years, the consumer would say the blend is worse because *they* have changed. Kakubin today is totally different to what it was ten years ago, because then it was a *mizuwari* drink and now it is a Highball. Maintaining quality is important, but improving quality is more important [there's the *kaizen* philosophy at work again] in process, cask management and the philosophy of maintaining brand quality.

'Whisky is random. It is always changing. We don't stick to a "recipe" because the whisky element will alway change. Each blend is new, every time.' Accept chance, craft flavour to suit the passing of time and changes in expectation, always improve.

How, though, can blends convert today's single-malt drinkers? Nikka's Blender's Bar in Tokyo, where you can sit down and make your own with the different component blocks, is one innovative way forward. The other is closer relationships with the bartending world globally – Suntory's Toki and Hibiki Harmony have both specifically targeted that community, while Nikka's From The Barrel not only works closely with the on-trade but has been made specifically to appeal to a malt drinker.

Help may come from an unlikely source. Grain whisky is no longer seen as the adulterant of single malt but as a whisky style with its own complexities. Nikka's two, Gotemba's three, Suntory's The Chita all offer new characters in whisky. If grain is shown not to be the 'problem', then maybe blends are worth looking at.

There is another element to that randomness of which Shinji talked. If it were always the same, a computer could make a blend. It cannot. Whisky needs to be understood, corralled. It needs a blender who understands the quirks of climate and wood in order to make it special. Blenders are the interface between the random and the controlled.

TASTING NOTES

The brand that started the whole shebang back in the 1930s was **Kakubin (40% ABV)**. In fact, you could argue that it was also the brand that kicked the category back into life when the Highball was rediscovered. Kaku is a mixing whisky. It performs best when it is served as a *mizuwari* or Highball. There's banana and bubblegum on the nose, along with a lick of cream and fat grain. The palate is drier, with a distinct bite on the finish.

Suntory has recently launched two other brands aimed at the mixing/cocktail market. **Toki (43% ABV)** is all dried apricots, citrus zest, and succulent grain, with a creamy pineapple and pear palate that expands with water into umami-like deliciousness.

Hibiki Harmony (43% ABV) is more serious, with red fruits: cherry, cranberry and a hint of incense in the

Japanese whisky was built on blends.

back. In the mouth it is luscious and rounded with all of those berry fruits and a cherry-blossom element. High-toned and clear.

The range also includes a **12-year-old (43% ABV)** which starts with spices, mango and pineapple before a gentle vanilla-led palate leads into a surprisingly tart finish coming from *umeshu* (plum liqueur) casks to wake the mouth up. The **17-year-old (43% ABV)** is brimful of citrus oils, cocoa, and deeply fruited with some light sherry and *mizunara*. Seamless. A limited (and expensive) **35-year-old (47% ABV)** has more overt *mizunara* and rancio waxiness. It's the smell of a *ryokan* mixed with apple syrup and black cherry, dried peels and balancing astringency.

Kirin's Fuji-Sanroku (50% ABV) is, unsurprisingly, grain-led, with that umami element giving texture to the palate. The nose has mature notes of black banana, praline and maraschino, while in the mouth there's an explosion of lilies and bluebells. A long, elegant blend.

Nikka's main thrust comes from **Super Nikka (43% ABV)**, which is less common in export markets but is, to my mind, one of Japan's most delicious blends. Mellow and sweet, there's plenty of vanilla, some toffee and those sweeter Miyagikyo-style fruits.

The world's bars are perhaps better acquainted with the dense **Nikka From The Barrel (51.4% ABV)**, a blend that is the polar opposite of Super Nikka. Here density rules: briary fruits, currant and smoke, which is brought forward with water, alongside a mineral edge, before the fruits crash back, adding a sweet-raisined quality to the finish. It's not subtle, but it is marvellous.

Newer is The **Nikka 12-year-old (43% ABV)**, which swings things back towards the Miyagikyo axis. More honeyed than Super Nikka, there's a light cassia note along with crisp apple, fresh-cut grass, pink grapefruit and surprisingly heavy floral elements. The palate is thick and gentle with the merest touch of smoke.

Three masters of their art, clockwise from opposite below: Nikka's Tadashi Sakuma, Suntory's Shinji Fukuyo, Kirin's Jota Tanaka.

INCENSE

My quest for the secrets of the *mizunara* scent involved sniffing whisky, then temples, and finally – via the Giant Panda Happy Train (I kid you not) – a visit to Baieido, Japan's oldest incense-maker, which has been trading on the same site in Sakai City, close to Osaka, for 16 generations, primarily making incense for temples.

The link between *mizunara*'s 'temple smell' and incense lies in molecules shared between the oak and the fungus-affected wood of *Aquilaria allagochea* or aloeswood (*jinko* in Japanese), which has been the key ingredient in temple incense since Buddhism arrived in Japan in 538 CE.

There are six grades, from *kyara* at the top to *sasora*. All share a highly complex, haunting aroma that combines all other woods and resins, flowers, tonka bean, cigar, dried fruit, leather. It is also insanely expensive. A gram of *kyara* will cost ¥20,000.

I went there for *jinko* but discovered that each example of the Baieido range will be a blend of up to 20 different ingredients, including sandalwood, cedar, frankincense, sandarac resin, benzoin resin, patchouli, clove, cinnamon, calamus root, galbanum resin, ambergris and mussel shell. Most will have the house's signature Borneo camphor in the mix.

All are ground, blended by smell, mixed with water into a paste, then extruded through what looks a like a noodle-making machine. The length of the stick is important as it measures time. A small stick will last for half an hour, 'the length of meditation'.

The sticks are then dried in the attic for three or four days, then sorted, packed and matured for six months. It's half-cigar factory, half-whisky lab. It needs understanding of aroma, blending, individuality, consistency, natural ingredients and the challenges they offer.

It was a fascinating world, a dim squeeze of a place in the backstreets where the scented dust of ages covered every surface. It's in the backstreets of our minds as well: the scents of fragrant woods and resins tap into a shared subconscious. Maybe incense-making was the first of the high olfactory arts.

To Nobuhiro Nakata, the firm's president, incense can be sweet like honey; sour like unripe plums; hot, like spices; salty like saltwater-soaked seaweed on a fire; and bitter, like a herbal medicine. The business was changing, however. 'We still make traditional incense,' he told me, 'but it is a smell of the past; we have to innovate. The young want light aromas: coffee or green tea – not their grandmother's house.' More links. More echoes.

The scent of *jin-ko* drifts out from every temple.

White Oak

江井ヶ嶋酒造

Osaka to Akashi

It's raining again as the three of us get the train from Osaka west to Akashi. As is now customary, no breakfast is taken, but there is time to fold ourselves plus bags into tiny tables in Akashi's station café and grab a soft, sweet sandwich. The rain redoubles its intensity. The taxi rank is beginning to flood. There's no sign of the sea, although it's possible we could be driving through it. I can sense Take is thinking of Plan Z as the downpour continues. This weather would test the patience of a saint.

Finally, as we turn off the main road, it begins to ease. Even on a heavy day like this there is also that widening of the light you get as you near the ocean. 'It's around here somewhere,' says the taxi driver. 'I think.' On one side of the road is a series of low buildings, their wooden planks charred and stained brown and black.

We drive around a deserted courtyard, then spot the modern building opposite with the sign 'White Oak Distillery'.

This is a distillery that is little known, one around which rumours swirl, whose whiskies pop out every so often and then just disappear.

Inside, we turn the meeting room into a left-luggage area. The seats are low and comfy. Tea is brought and a tall, thin, grey-haired man with a slightly distracted air walks in. He introduces himself as Mikio Hiraishi, whose family has owned this operation since 1888.

Signs at White Oak (Eigashima).

WHITE OAK

江
井
ケ
嶋
酒
造

Mikio Hiraishi seems reticent initially, but soon opens up. 'Eigashima was famous for its sake in the Edo period,' he says. 'Five breweries came together to form this firm, which was unusual at the time. The person who started it all had a lot of energy and spirit. I suppose these days we would call him a venture capitalist.' He grins his wide grin. It later transpires that he is talking about his great-grandfather, Urabe Yokichi.

'Anyway, for five years the sake made here was rated among the top ten in Japan. Then, from 1919, we started to produce other things – *shōchū*, for example – and the range of spirits began.' There are familiar themes here: the experienced producer seeing a market opening up, then beginning to diversify. In 1919, whisky would have been a logical route to take.

'I'm actually not sure when whisky distilling started,' he confesses. 'I can say it was definitely being made in 1964 in the Olympic time.' But wasn't a licence to make whisky taken out in 1919? 'Oh yes' – that grin again – 'we had the licence, but as far as I know we didn't make it. We did have whisky brands, though; we'd buy in spirit and blend it here. The date of the licence does, however, mean that theoretically we were the first whisky distillery.' He's not pushing the assertion that Japanese whisky started here, however. As with Iwai's thwarted plans at Settsu Shozu (see page 42), you can't help but think, what if?

It's easy (if wrong) to think of White Oak as being the dilettante of Japanese whisky: making it when they want, stopping, starting, never quite committing to the cause (whisky-lovers can tend to have a rather fundamentalist outlook at times). I'd prefer to think of them as pragmatic. 'You know well that there was a period when it was hard to sell whisky,' Hiraishi continues. 'There was no recognition of its quality and people weren't willing to buy, so we stopped.'

The distillery was upgraded in 1984, but that was hardly the best time to start venturing into whisky. You cut your cloth. Surely though, the boom means there's more being made now?

'Now we have stopped making *shōchū* and are only making sake and whisky here. Oh and *umeshu* [plum liqueur].' You can almost see him

White Oak had the first licence for making whisky in Japan.

counting his fingers in his head as he checks things off. 'And wine; we have a winery in Yamanashi close to Hakushu. Oh, and some mirin.'

So whisky is more important now? He wraps his arms around his chest and laughs. 'It always depends on time and history, but now? Sure. I think the recognition of whisky is being pushed more now, so it is becoming more important to the firm, so, yes we are making more, but gradually!' There's a sense that nothing round here has ever happened quickly.

As is habitual at Japanese distilleries, the old stills are outside. These are minuscule, pocket-sized pots: 'From 1964,' he explains. What style did you make? He rocks with invisible mirth. 'I don't know! I'm not sure what it was in those days.'

By the looks of them, it would have been pretty heavy.

Inside the facility things start fairly conventionally. There's a modern Bühler mill, the barley comes from Crisp in Portgordon in 1,000-kilo (1-tonne) sacks and is lightly peated, but then it gets weird. In a nice way, you understand, but distinctly weird.

You enter on a mezzanine floor facing two tanks. One looks like a mash tun, but isn't. The other one, looking like a receiving vat, is. It transpires that the first is for saccharification to take place. Then it's sent across to the second tank where it settles and is filtered. Why do you do it this way? I ask Hiraishi. 'It's just what happened,' he replies. 'We had no help or information, so this is what we started to do.'

江井ヶ嶋酒造

There's another tank that has water cascading over it, flooding the floor below. This, it turns out, is where White Oak's own yeast is being grown. That water is the tank's temperature control. The wort (clear) and yeast are then pumped into one of four stainless-steel washbacks and left to ferment for between three to five days.

The stills, small and angular, seem straightforward, but the spirit is collected in a spirit still that sits on the floor (a first for me) and is collected as new-make at a very low strength: between 55 and 60% ABV.

Production remains tiny, only 48,000 litres a year, but is steadily being upped. Evidence for the new focus can be seen in the rows of casks sitting below: fresh bourbon and some new 220-litre (*c.*58 US gallons) sherry casks, coopered in Japan. There's an even wider variety in the warehouse: refill American oak, old sherry, recharred *shōchū* casks. Cognac, tequila. Most exciting is a cask made from another oak native to Japan, *konara (Quercus serrata)*, which has been trialled as a 'finishing' cask; a 15-year-old was released in 2013.

We walk over to taste the current bottlings. As production and stock levels are limited – currently the oldest stock is eight years old – these are eked out in tiny quantities and small bottles, mainly as single malt (often finished), but there have been blends as well, including a somewhat controversial one that also included molasses spirit, meaning it could not be called 'whisky' under EU regulations. All sell out quickly.

I ask Hiraishi-san what his plans are for a decade's time. 'I'd want to specialize in single malt because that is representative of what we

Low wines boiling inside the spirit still (opposite). The production of whisky is increasing at White Oak (below).

make, but we have to build up the stock. This is a big change for us. Pre-1989 this was all second-tier whisky. We are finding our way.' He grins again. 'You asked me about "Japanese character" earlier. I'm not sure I can answer.

'You see, in *shōchū* and sake we have a history, but not in whisky. There's still no real contact with other distilleries, therefore there's this element of trial and error. Remember, when we started we had no idea!' He laughs again. His frankness is refreshing.

There's an improvisatory air about White Oak. It does things its own way because it feels like it. Although lines of communication are now open with Chichibu and Hombo you get the feeling that this approach won't change much.

Outside the rain has passed and the smell of the sea reasserts itself. Does the ocean have any influence, I ask? 'Oh yes,' he replies. 'Things get rusty!' We're heading across to the sake *kura* (brewery), with its amazingly textured timbered cladding, past the statue of his great-grandfather. 'In sake you have to train in beer. Whisky is similar, but it's also easier to make! If you master sake with good training then you can make whisky.'

Hiraishi-san is one of the great optimists.

The sake *kura* at White Oak (below). Mikio Hiraishi, whose family has owned the company since 1888 (opposite).

江井ヶ嶋酒造

TASTING NOTES

White Oak sits next to the sea.

The White Oak new-make is medium weight with a slight yeasty edge to it that gives way to lifted esters, some red fruit and a touch of polished brass in the background. The feel in the mouth is clean and sweet, with just a tickle of smoke at the end. Limited production in the past has left them with little to draw on, but bottlings, while limited in nature, are becoming more regular. Of the two available at the time of visiting, the **Akashi three-year-old** (50% ABV) shows a bready, sourdough note on the nose (that yeastiness in the new-make, perhaps) with light oak, pear drops, green apple and lime. The palate was more strawberry-like, with a grating of nutmeg on the end. It shows real promise.

The **Akashi eight-year-old** (50% ABV) was aged in ex-sherry and it shows, with big dried-fruit aromas (dates especially) along with some tofu, then oak. The cask makes the palate seem quite showy although the spirit is light and slightly shy. Some cask-driven flavours of chocolate and dry-roasted spices round it off.

Akashi to Kyoto

We taxi back into town where, either thanks to a tip-off or Take's highly tuned senses, we end sitting at a counter eating *akashiyaki*, Akashi-style octopus balls. I love the Kansai speciality *takoyaki*, a morsel of octopus encased in a bite-sized batter ball, then smothered in *okonomiyaki* sauce and mayonnaise with flakes of bonito waving gently on the surface. I'd insisted on some last night, in fact.

Akashi has its own variant. Egg-based batter rather than flour. No sauce, just *dashi* as a dip. Pillowy, soft, gentle, just slightly bouncy. I'm converted. 'One more board?' I plead, but we have to get to Kyoto.

That evening, I caught up with some old friends, David Croll and his wife, Noriko Kakuda. After some excellent – but whisky-free – *kaiseki* we reverted to type and headed into town in search of a nightcap. Such wanderings have been a staple of our relationship. Over the years Croll-san and I have drunk in many of the country's finest and most obscure places; we've bathed together, sat *zazen*, learned about sake, talked whisky. He now owns a gin distillery in Kyoto. As you do.

'Let's do the monk bar,' he says. While a monk running a bar seems to contradict the Buddhist precepts, Bozu Bar, next to Honnoji temple, is one of a number across Japan. It turns out that owner Takahide Haneda and I had met at a tasting I'd done at Kanga-an temple, which also has a bar. Buddhism can be remarkably fluid.

A bar does seem an unusual departure, though. 'I could have been stuck in a monastery and hidden from people,' Haneda replies, 'whereas I should be trying to help them, and serve the community. A bar seemed to be the best place that people can come and talk to me about their problems.' He gives a sermon each day and, on leaving, guests are given a leaflet that helps to continue the conversation they'd had with Haneda-san.

I wonder if alcohol is necessarily the best way to help people face their problems, but then remember that while this might not be a great idea in Scotland, it seems to work perfectly well in Japan.

NATURE

It's easy to be seduced by Japan and view it through Hello Kitty-hued spectacles that allow you to see a place of calm and tranquillity, of cherry blossoms and geishas, one where tradition is worshipped, everything is slow and polite; a remnant of a slower, gentler world in which nature is revered. The reality is different. The geishas may exist, the *sakura* (cherry blossom) falls, but Japan is also a highly industrialized society. Its cities are loud and consumer-driven, their streets hung with cables and lit at night by a dead fluorescent glow.

At some point in any of the discussions with the makers on this trip, the talk turned to nature: the importance of the seasons, about being close to it, respecting, reflecting and being inspired by it, the use of natural products like clay, mulberry, water, barley, wood and so on. They follow *haiku* master Basho's advice: 'The first lesson for the artist is to learn to follow nature, to be one with nature … To understand the pine … go to the pine.'

They are the exception. In Japan, nature is tamed, obliterated, held at arm's length. I'd seen it at Chita, but as I knew Chita was in an industrial site there was little surprise. It was brought home more sharply at White Oak. The romantic location shot Take and I had envisaged – distillery, beach, sea, to contrast with the establishing woodland shots of the others – was virtually impossible. The sea was blocked off. The beach was concrete.

I understand the need for tsunami defences, having travelled through the zone of the post-Tohoku earthquake where towns were reduced to piles of matchwood. There were cars left on top of a block of flats, a fishing boat lay in the main street and there were pools of stinking, oily water, collapsed houses, rags of curtains fluttering in the breeze. The current magic fix of concrete 'tetrapods' is not, however, the solution.

The encasing of the coast had started long before that. It was part of Japan's post-war governments' project radically to shift the nation's destiny, which wreaked environmental devastation on the country and was a brutal escalation of a process that had been ongoing for hundreds of years as the dangerous, unpredictable wild was pushed back.

In *Japan and the Culture of the Four Seasons* (2013), Haruo Shirane writes, '[In Japan] harmony with nature is not an inherent closeness to primary nature … but a result of close ties to secondary nature'. Think of it: poetry, tea ceremony, flower-arranging, gardening,

the clipped trees in the city streets. All involve nature being ordered, codified, manipulated by man into a better, cleaner simulacrum.

'The Japanese attitude to nature [is that] it must be remade,' writes Arturo Silver in *The Great Mirror (The Donald Richie Reader)*. 'In a word, "our nature is art, to perceive what is made and remake it".' The apparent national reverence for nature is in fact a reverence for an impossibly perfect, tamed nature. One step removed.

There have been 1,000 dams constructed since 1946 and today, only two of Japan's 102 main rivers are undammed. Most are silted up. New dams are still being built despite there being no need for them, and corruption within the public works process bulldozes aside any objections, of which there are few. In 1997, *New Scientist* reported that only three of the country's 142 larger rivers still had their natural banks. Most riverbeds have been concreted over to stop flooding, although by speeding up the water flow, concreting helps to cause it, while more than 60 per cent of the coastline has been reclaimed. There is a constant battle between planned forestry and the last remaining old growth.

Environmental degradation is everywhere, resulting in massive species and habitat loss. Nature is enclosed in gardens and parks. Concrete covers everything.

The wild is important, not just in terms of biodiversity, but psychologically. We need the disordered and random, places in which to get lost. It shows us that life is not predictable and linear, but confused, tangled, full of dead ends and new vistas. Having a method is important, but inspiration and innovation only come by accepting the need for chance – the willingness to step off that safe highway and see what is there.

Craft is enmeshed deeply in this because it is inextricably tied up in natural processes, but that wild thinking is under threat. All of the makers spoke of problems, a loss of interest, a lack of new blood. Like Japan's environment, their position is precarious.

Japan's coastline is encased in concrete.

Return to Kyoto

As today's schedule only had an afternoon visit to Seikado planned, Take decided it would make sense to head out west to see the Matsunoo shrine. He's long since ceased to be 'the cameraman' and is now guide, confidante, sounding-board for some of my more outrageous stumbling thoughts, and friend. He got this mad quest from the off and is now a partner in its denouement – wherever it takes us.

The three of us watch as a small boy swings the thick rope in front of the main shrine, trying to make the heavy bell rattle and clatter. We're here because this is not only a major shrine, but one where, at each point of the rice harvest and sake-making process, brewers come to pray (there is no separate shrine for whisky distillers; they're too new on the scene, so they tend to share sake ones). There's also an extraordinary set of gardens designed in 1975 by Mirei Shigemori and, following on from my ranting about wildness and secondary nature, the whole compound backs onto a mountain.

Legend has it that Matsunoo was founded in 701 when a local chief saw a tortoise (a symbol of long life) drinking from a spring. Worship of its rocks, falls and water could possibly pre-date that. Good water means health, a quality ingredient for sake brewing, miso-making and agriculture. The shrine is in some way a walk through Japanese history; the gardens are ancient and wild, with rocks like the top of the mountain; there is a gentle curving stream that snakes past rocks and azaleas to represent the height of grace and creativity of the Heian period (794–1185), and a phoenix-shaped pool representing in some way the Showa Era of 1926–89 (not that I discerned why), in which massive rocks sit close to a fountain indicating age and eternal youth.

I am more intrigued by the path that leads away from this controlled environment through a *torii* gate into the woods and the mountainside. It ends at the waterfall at whose foot the tortoise was said to have lived. There's thick moss on the stone lanterns, the *tōrō*. Crows call in the trees, minuscule mushrooms sprout from crevices in bark. The place has presence, not in an overly religious way – Shinto as far as I can tell veers away from over-religiosity. It's just there, an unheard hum of spirits, of *kami*, underpinning life, ensuring that things continue. It seems a special location where elements combine in the right balance. It's a recalibration.

We head back into the city to meet with David and Noriko and our appointment with Seikado.

The snaking river at the Matsunoo shrine.

PEWTER

I trust Croll-san implicitly. I trust Noriko more, so when she said that a pewter workshop she'd found fitted the craft bill I was happy to go along, though I wasn't quite sure what to expect. There's not much pewterware in the UK, other than dusty old pint pots in dusty old pubs. Its days seem to have passed.

Seikado's shop/workshop is in the centre of Kyoto, on Teramachi-dori, the heart of an area which, in a city that prides itself on being the repository of all that is most refined about traditional Japan, is dedicated, it seem, to little else. We walk past old bookshops, a bamboo workshop, stores selling items for the tea ceremony. Nishiharu, where I've bought woodblock prints, is down the street, while Kyoto's most famous soba house, Kawamichi-ya, is a block away, likewise the city's finest *ryokan*, the sublimely elegant Hiiragiya. If those are the neighbours, this will be something special.

The whole shop glitters as you enter. There are exquisite flasks and drinking cups, bowls, tea caddies and vases. The owner, Genpei Yamanaka, comes out from the back room. He's young, with a shaved head, a piercing gaze and loose-fitting work clothes. He is the seventh generation of a firm that was established 180 years ago on this site.

Pewter arrived in Japan from China between the sixth and eighth centuries, he explains, and until the end of the Tokugawa Era in 1867 it was for the wealthy. 'We started around this crossover period, so have always made a range of goods – everything from objects for shrines and temples to the tea ceremony and sake.

'Pewter was traditionally used for warm sake. Although the drink is acidic, pewter will never go rusty, so it was more appropriate than other metals. It also helps to mellow the sake. Each metal has its own smell, particularly when it is warm, and pewter's matches that of warm sake.'

I don't immediately think of metal as having a smell, but then I recall the dull, bitter notes reminiscent of old copper coins found in some old Scotch, the mineral sharpness of steel. Maybe those old guys chose pewter mugs for their ale because of its qualities, not because they were cheap. I resolve to try whether pewter works with whisky as well.

Pewter's advantage is that it is extremely malleable. It has a low melting point, so vessels can be made either by pouring into a mould or, as here, by forging. It also has the unusual quality of 'soldering' to itself when two edges are hammered together.

He crouches down beside one of the tree trunks used as worktables and picks up a small triangular piece. 'Look. You can shape it with a hammer and a stake. When you hammer it, the pewter becomes harder. Now,' he picks up a round-ended hammer, 'using this you can add a different texture.' As he strikes it, tiny moons appear. 'Now,' another tool, 'I can incise it, or use this' – another one with a stippled head – 'to give this effect.' The clear surface is now covered with coils and ripples like the viscimetric effect when water is added to whisky.

One of his apprentices is quietly working at finishing a sake flask. 'That will take about four days from start to finish', Yamanaka-san says. 'A cup will be two or three days' work.'

How long is the apprenticeship? 'I was with my father for ten years.' And are younger people coming into this? 'Out of the five we have, four are in their 20s or early 30s. The fifth is 70!' How many workshops are like this? 'In Japan? There might be ten making pewter goods in the country. No-one is doing the same as we are, though.'

Does that make it precarious? He fixes me with that calm gaze.

'Pewter is small-scale in terms of traditional crafts in Japan. There are 100 potters in Kyoto alone! In fact, I'd say that ceramics is actually a little behind the times and not innovating so quickly.'

So change is necessary?

'It's vital. We have had to make big changes in the way we run the business. We used only to sell through a wholesaler, then department stores. Now it is only this shop and via the web. It allows me to target a specific market, and the profits are better.'

Was that a difficult shift?

'Well, there were complaints, but it makes business sense. We have to change – and the designs have to as well. Consumers' tastes are changing quicker, so the product cycle is quicker too. We have to strike that balance between keeping pace with that and respecting tradition. That textured effect isn't really traditional. Sake has changed as well; it used to be sipped warm so the containers were small. Now it is usually cold, so we have to redesign the flask. You have to have patience to do this work, but also be willing slowly to move the tradition forward.'

Genpei Yamanaka, the preserver of the art of pewter.

We go back into the store. He picks up a flask, seems to weigh it. Nods slightly. 'It's the feeling in your hand that's important.'

He is, of course, right. Craft isn't just measured by the eye, but by the hand, or the nose, the palate – and you could say the heart. It's functional, therefore it demands engagement. The further it is pushed to the margins the more detached it becomes and the more fragile its future. Japanese crafts are being saved by tourism and export, by Japan's image and reputation abroad.

Craft exists in every country and culture. The pressures felt by makers in Japan are the same as anywhere where mass-production and an obsession with the new is marginalizing traditional techniques. This is also hardly new a phenomenon. It's what William Morris was fighting against in the 19th century. Why then is it so important now, and why in Japan? It is important because it keeps us in touch with the idea of making, of the natural world, of care and patience, and the benefits of slowness.

It's important in Japan because, despite the detached view of nature, its complexities are inextricably entwined – perhaps subconsciously – in the sense of being Japanese. Here its influence goes beyond 'just' making and has created a whole aesthetic that is everywhere, from typefaces to shop displays. The way a purchase will be carefully wrapped, the manner in which you hand over a credit card or receive your change: all are based on a craft approach. It is there in smell and flavour and taste.

It's appropriate maybe that this dip into that world ends in Kyoto, a city I love that bit more with each visit as another door is opened, another facet revealed. It can go in any direction. It might end up with that geisha and her question about potatoes, or sipping cocktails at the magnificent bar, Rocking Chair. You could drink oxidized sake in a bar run by an Israeli, or drink Manhattans made by a self-taught retired greengrocer at Bar Quasimodo. The day could be spent 'listening' to incense, walking round endless temples, or crate-digging for obscure vinyl. It could be jazz tonight or Zen. Kyoto is more restrained than Osaka or Tokyo but it is not boring.

'Let's go out,' says Take. 'I'll show you some bars.' So starts another dive into the lesser-known parts of the city. First stop is Bar Bunkyu. Up a darkened pathway to a room with one huge table that might fit 12. There

Creating textures on pewter.

are no bottles on show, no menu. Ask for a drink and the bartender goes into the back, brings the bottles he needs, makes the drinks, and stashes the bottles out of sight again. By that time you're chatting with everyone else round the table. It's very un-Japanese. It is very, very un-Kyoto.

There's time for another. In a rundown building opposite a side-street shrine is Kazu's, not that you'd know what lies behind the unmarked door on the top floor. Candle flames throw stars on the woodwork. It's like some old Soho basement 'club' or illicit den on the Lower East Side before things got all gentrified. There's minimal techno and fine whiskies. We can relax. It doesn't shut until 5am.

The last leg looms. Finally, the road leads north.

A selection of pewter sake ware.

WABI-SABI

I was trying to avoid the whole *wabi-sabi* thing, to be honest, having figured it's just too hard to shoehorn the concept into whisky. *Shibui* seemed a more natural fit. It still nagged away, though. What is it? 'Very difficult,' is the standard response, accompanied by an intake of breath, a smile, a shake of the head. My friend Maki once pointed out a tree in the garden of Kanga-an temple. 'See how the leaves are turning? That's *wabi-sabi*.' I got that. Then someone else said something that seemed completely the opposite.

Maybe it is one of the Japanese things one will never understand. Maybe no-one does. It is close to *shibui* but from my reading of it, it has a little more to do with age, or rather the nature of time passing as well as that understated, humble, elegant simplicity. You see? Not easy.

Anyway, there I was in Seikado holding a simple, plain sake flask which Yamanaka-san's grandfather had made. It had a gentle weight, a dull, almost blue patina. Its surface contained dings and dents where it had been grasped, or fallen during long-lost nights of drinking. You could almost feel the warmth of the old man's hand emanating from its surface. It glowed internally, as if it absorbed light, then receded to sit

quietly in the shadows. I look at Take. '*Wabi-sabi*?' He nods. 'Yes,' says Yamanaka. 'He loved this. It has *wabi-sabi*.' And your pieces? He smiles. 'Maybe in a hundred years.'

I pass it over. He runs his fingers over the surface. 'Using pewter means you get dents, but if this had been made from copper it would not have aged like this. It has the feel of age, the respect for age, it brings back memories of my ancestors.'

Looking at it brought to mind lines from *In Praise of Shadows* (1977), Junichiro Tanizaki's paean to Japanese aesthetics. 'We find it hard to be really at home with things that shine and glitter,' he writes. 'We begin to enjoy [silver] only when the lustre has worn off, when it has begun to take on a dark, smoky patina…a glow that comes from being touched again and again… [its] beauty not in the thing itself but in a pattern of shadows, the light and the darkness that one thing against another creates.'

The flask had this quality.

So, deep breath, here's my take on *wabi-sabi*. It's about appreciating the humble and organic by embracing the unpredictability of natural processes. As Tanizaki writes, it exists in and welcomes the shad-

ows. It celebrates the unconventionally beautiful, and simple; it appreciates that flaws are integral to beauty, because they show an acceptance of time passing. *Wabi-sabi* reflects on this and sees the joy in a falling leaf or petal, the bitterness at the end of the season which is still a positive quality. The question is, does whisky have it?

Not automatically. It doesn't simply appear when every whisky is, say, 25 years old, but there are those that carry their age in a certain way: where the flavours, rather than becoming heavier or woodier, evolve into something both aromatically pure and deep – resins and fresh fruits, honey and polished wood. They are whiskies that whisper about the time which has passed. They can be found.

I was thinking of the sensory assault of the canyons of Osaka, and how Japan with its multifunctional toilets (oh, for a Toto toilet at home!) and *kawaii* obsession, its cat cafés and shouting billboards, its cheesy electronic noise and pet shops open at 5am selling miniature dogs to drunken businessmen to give to their hostesses who then sell the dogs back to the shop. Where has *wabi-sabi* gone in this addictive, bonkers, never-never land? Maybe it resides in those quiet

bars, those meditation caves in the neon rockface of modern life, where you can sip on something that glows internally, that speaks of time.

Yamanaka-san's grandfather's flask exhibits *wabi-sabi*.

Yoichi

余市蒸溜所

Kyoto to Sapporo

It's time for Take and me to say goodbye to Yuki and, missing breakfast again, make a quick dash to see the stone gardens at Tenryu-ji. Shades and textures of moss make islands out of which a pine rises; a chessboard is obscured or revealed. In the main garden, recumbent rocks, circular patterns like raindrops in the ground, pulses of thought, energy waves. All is movement and stillness, contemplation and creativity.

No time to think longer. We have the train back to Kyoto, a bus to Osaka, then a flight to Sapporo, where we're met by Nikka's Emiko Kaji and chief blender Tadashi Sakuma. After checking in to the hotel, Take and I do another quick orientation sprint around the city's grid of wide streets and into the town hall in search of some evidence of the island's original inhabitants, the Ainu. There's nothing.

The official line is that Hokkaido was only settled in the 1870s. It barely even appeared on Japanese maps until the end of the 18th century, when there would be just a sketch of the south coast, and the rest would be void. It was Ezo ('Place of Foreigners') or the more poetic Kari no Michi ('Route of the Wild Geese').

It had by then been home to the Paleoasiatic Ainu for millennia. Hokkaido's like America or Canada before the white men came, Japan's frontier, settlers meeting with indigenous peoples, changing the landscape, introducing arable crops, ranching and dairy farms. The settlers advance and the Ainu, with their belief in an interdependent world where gods, animals, plants and men are equals sharing the same territory, slip away almost out of sight.

Hokkaido, with its old-growth *mizunara*, yew, cypress and cedar, rich seas, owls, wintering cranes, bear, volcanoes and thick snow, is seen as a place of opportunity and exploitation. Like many zones on the margins – deserts, western coasts, extremes of north or south – it attracted (and still does) dreamers and misfits. It had space – this island of 78,500sq km (30,300

square miles) still only supports a population of five million – to breathe, think and dream.

It's also the place where, finally, we can get to grips with Masataka Taketsuru, the last of Japanese whisky's founding fathers. The brilliant young chemist was sent off to Glasgow to find whisky's secrets and returned with them, plus a Scottish wife. He had a partnership with Shinjiro Torii, but they fell out and his pilgrimage/departure/self-imposed exile (I'm still not sure which) was here to Hokkaido, where he founded Nikka and took on his former boss.

I want to try and get into his head, to find out why here, about how his vision was different to Torii's, about his attachment to Scotland and how, slowly, he cut himself free. But that's tomorrow.

'A quick bite?' says Take.

'But we're on our way to dinner,' I reply.

'Yes, but this is special. Just one plate …' We go into a modern little restaurant. Two bowls with some light dipping sauce, bright greens and thin slivers of crunchy-textured pale flesh. 'We call it *gutsu*,' he says. 'It's the intestines of cows, served raw.' My eyebrow must have flickered. 'It has to be clean,' he reassures me. No kidding.

We're hooking up with a BBC film crew who are doing a series on the history of Scotch. As we sit with our hosts they bowl in, complete with presenter/Scottish acting legend David Hayman. 'The *Daily Record* has come out for independence!' he cries as way of a greeting. As I'm engulfed in tales of the Brexit fallout, I realize how out of touch I've become. Quick calls home, trying to console my daughter, my wife searching for Irish ancestors. I need to get back.

Our banquet is accompanied by Nikka Black Highballs. 'Mix whisky? Never!' says Hayman. Postdinner, I take them to the Nikka bar at Sapporo's main crossroads. There are flights of single malts, vatted malts and, because I'm stubborn, a From the Barrel Highball. I'll convince the bugger. 'This is a blend?' he says. 'Wow. That's a good drink.' Out of such small victories whisky was built.

Hokkaido: A boisterous welcome (opposite), Sapporo's ubiquitous TV tower (above left) and rich surrounding seas (above right).

YOICHI

白
州
蒸
溜
所

Early next morning, Take and I go to the fish market, but unlike Tokyo's equivalent, Tsukiji, you have to watch the auctions from a distance. There are, however, restaurants, which means keeping my promise made to Momma-san at Chichibu to have *kegane kani-miso*: 'crab brain' at its most extreme, a head-clearing distillation of the sea. There's also *kegane* itself and *uni* (Hokkaido's sea urchin is famed) and popping *ikura* (salmon eggs). The finest breakfast you could imagine. Fortified, the taste of the sea in our heads, we're ready for the drive west to Yoichi.

The coast doesn't emerge slowly, but leaps at you at the end of a tunnel – the grey ocean, steep cliffs, rank upon rank of mountains slowly walking into the waves, the light bright and cool. Through Otaru, to Yoichi town and the distillery, with its castellated stone gatehouse and, again, a sudden expansion of the scene. On the left, the low distillery buildings, opposite, capped in scarlet, the massive kilns topped with pagoda roofs.

Guides wander about with loudspeakers. It's early, but already the car park is full of buses. In 2014, Japan's main TV station, NHK, started a 40-week morning soap opera (of the 15-minute kind called *asadora*) based on the love story between Taketsuru and his wife, Rita. The 'Massan effect', from the soap opera of the same name, saw sales of Nikka going through the roof and stock levels becoming even more depleted. In 2015, a million people visited the site.

Yoichi was the starting point for many of us. That first glass was part of a blind flight of whiskies at *Whisky Magazine*'s Best of the Best in 2001 and ended up winning the whole competition. It may have been a small event, but its repercussions were enormous. It made the whisky world take notice of Japan; more importantly, it gave the Japanese distillers the boost in confidence they needed to start an export strategy.

It was new for all of us, the flavours so familiar yet different, a remix, a palimpsest. There was smoke, yes, but the way it worked with the oils was different: the brightness and intensity of the top notes; the ordered manner in which the flavours presented themselves. It was rich and deep but somehow clear and cool simultaneously. We didn't know about multi-stream blending; we simply tasted and were captivated.

Before we start to walk around, let's try and get our get heads around Taketsuru. To read his mind we have to look also at the supporting cast of a tale that has taken on the qualities of myth. We need to look at Rita, who wasn't just 'the wife', but central to the story.

She was cultured, highly educated. Her sister was studying medicine, her late father had been a doctor, but as her fiancé had died in the Second World War Rita was conceivably looking at a lifetime in genteel middle-class Glasgow, the maiden aunt who looked after an ageing parent. Masataka, perhaps, was a second chance.

Glasgow itself is a character. Taketsuru arrived in December 1918. On 'Black Friday', 31 January 1919, 10,000 troops, backed up with tanks, were sent to the city to quell what some felt was the start of a Bolshevik revolution. He was flung into a febrile political atmosphere, surrounded by increasingly empowered women. Three months after Black Friday, arriving back from Elgin he wrote: '... Glasgow is my town'.

Later in life, he wrote how getting married would be one way for him to stay in Scotland. Rita's reply was that his dream was to make whisky in Japan and that they should go. What does the marriage say? That they were in love, headstrong, independent, impulsive, rebellious, not afraid to flout convention.

Yoichi's gigantic kiln buildings – no longer in use.

He—they—could make a radical difference in Japan. In time, he did. In 1934, chastened by the perceived demotion from being Japan's only whisky distiller to being made the head of Kotobukiya brewery, he resigned and they moved north—far north and west, here to Yoichi to establish what was to become Nikka. The money came in part from Osakan investors, the parents of a middle-class couple to whose children Rita had taught piano. They were a team.

But why here? There was good agricultural land (albeit with a short growing season), there was peat in the Ishikiri Valley, and plentiful water. There were also apples, because his first venture was called Dai Nippon Kaju ('Great Japanese Juice Company') so not as to offend Torii. The NI and KA from the original name would become the company name in the 1950s.

But why specifically build Yoichi next to the cold ocean, alongside the fishing boats? We know that one of his investors had connections in the town, but the choice of such a spot seems almost as if he were building a Scotland of the mind. He and Rita were happiest in Scotland when in Campbeltown, at Hazelburn. Maybe this location was a gift to Rita at some level. It wasn't the most sensible place to build, as far from markets as you could imagine. Here, for me, is Taketsuru's romantic streak winning over the pragmatic.

It's why I don't wholly buy the inference that he chose it solely because it was the nearest place he could find to Scotland. Since the mid-19th cen-

Memories of Taketsuru.

Taketsuru still watches over his first distillery.

tury, Scottish distilleries had been built next to roads, railways, ferry ports, harbours. The days of a location being hidden for moonshining, or rural, on a farm close to crops, had long receded. A different sensibility about place had developed. Transport links were key. He'd have learned that.

There is peat on Honshu. Barley can be grown there; there is water – and there is a market. Hokkaido's climate is different, but could that really have been the sole reason for moving so far, so north, so west?

We're in the (now-disused) kiln. 'We still cut some Ishikari peat for show,' says Sakuma. Great flat slabs of it lie in a pile. 'It stopped in the 1970s, when the market was growing too rapidly and we didn't have the capacity to kiln everything on site.' Today, Yoichi is using mainly Scottish malt (from different maltings, which itself adds variations) in three style: unpeated, medium-, and heavy-peated. In typical Japanese style, these are then blended in different ratios to produce an even wider range of flavour possibilities.

I'm looking at the architecture. Each kiln took one tonne but they are significantly larger than is needed. Either they were built in anticipation of an increase in production (but Sakuma said they couldn't cope) or the high roof gave greater air circulation and so a better control over the smoke. This is a distillery built on tradition but also diversity.

There's a new Bühler mill, but tradition kicks in at the mash tun (which holds between four and six tonnes) that still has an old 'rake and plough' system. 'An old man told us that Taketsuru said: "Wort must be clear, yeast must be brewer's, and the distilling must be cold",' says Sakuma. 'Those are the fundamentals we carry forward.' They move forward, but only somehow with his blessing. Here, change is adaptation rather than a radical shift.

That direction to make clear wort is an issue. Rake and plough mash tuns have curved arms (the rakes), which move through the mash like swimmers doing the crawl (the plough). This disturbs the bed and increases the likelihood of husks getting through and that nutty cereal element emerging.

'We circulate the first water so that it is double-filtered,' Sakuma explains, with a sight glass as per Mars Shinshu being employed. 'It has to be clear enough to see your hand,' he says, demonstrating.

There are 20 washbacks, though currently only six are used. The ferments are long – up to five days. 'The time is right because of the lactobacilli. After three days they start to increase and as well as esters being created, the pH decreases, which is important for distillation [the lower the pH, the more acidic the wash, which helps to clean up copper and remove heavier elements]. The balance of amino acids is also changed. The length also depends on the yeast we select.

'We use Taketsuru's original strain, and there's an ale yeast, and Mauri distiller's yeast. Taketsuru would have possibly used a beer yeast from the Sapporo brewery [which opened in 1876]. These are used singly or in combination.' More diversity.

There's another facet to Yoichi not seen perhaps at any other distillery anywhere in the world. Again, it comes back to Taketsuru's edicts. Its stills sit high up on a brick platform. Under them are ovens. A pile of coal sits alongside. The stills aren't just direct-fired, but coal-fired.

'We don't want to change the quality,' Sakuma says, 'and the coal fires are important for the body. If we used another flame the heat would be stable and that is the key.' A coal fire is unpredictable, hard to control and creates more hot spots on the base of the still; the temperature is between 800° and 1,000°C (1,472° and 1,832°F). If managed properly, this develops deep, roasted flavours as the wash drags against those hot spots. Let it stick, though, and it burns. Gas gives control, but coal means the stillman must constantly anticipate. The fires help in the creation of Yoichi's depth, as does the steep downward angle to the lyne arms and worm tubs, both restricting copper conversation and pushing the distillate in a heavy, oily direction.

The stillhouse is about adding muscle to those fruits created by the long ferment and clear wort. In the corner is one small pot still. 'That was the only still,' says Sakuma. 'Taketsuru used it for mash and spirit distillation, right up until the first expansion in 1966.' It would, potentially, have been heavier again.

'Yoichi should be true to tradition,' he adds. 'Miyagikyo is the modern approach. We have to make them both distinct.' That's a blender talking. Again, there are multiple streams being created here, for use in the blends and also the malts, by utilizing different peating levels, ferment times, yeast combinations and cut points: a higher cut for the lighter style, and lower to capture heavier phenols in the peaty variants. In the warehouse

'So clear you can see your hand' – the sight glass at the mash tun.

there are new-oak, ex-bourbon, puncheons, re-charred, ex-sherry and refill casks. Again, diversity.

Hokkaido's long, extremely cold winters and warm summers also impact on maturation and the flavours created. What else, though, did it do to Taketsuru's mind?

We walk around the house where he and Rita lived. It's as if they have just popped out: the pickle jar in the kitchen, his clothes in the wardrobe, books on the shelf. One room is like my maiden aunt's house in Perth: piano, old brown furniture, heavy carpets. Next door, a classic Japanese room: wooden floors, *tatami*, low tables. There was always this split, a Japanese sensibility but also this pull to Scotland. Respect for his teachers retained.

The Nikka logo of a medieval-looking chap with a feathered bonnet is meant to represent William Phaup Lowry, the leading blender in nine-teenth-century Scotland, the man who bankrolled William Buchanan (Black & White), and who patented the treatment of sherry casks. Was he an inspiration to Taketsuru? In 1925, when his first distillates at Yamazaki didn't work, Taketsuru went back to Scotland to seek advice from his mentor, Peter Innes. Here, in the north, always looking west.

For me, he didn't only come here because of perfect conditions. Nei-ther did he come to hide, but to have space to develop his vision, to think deeply about what his 'Japaneseness' meant, Torii's vision of something lighter, how it sat with his adherence to the lessons of his masters. This divergence in approach helped to create Japanese whisky as a category. Hokkaido becomes an active participant, thanks to the impact of its

geography but also its space. Sometimes to innovate and move things forward you have to step away from the tracks of convention and head into the wilderness. That's where the ideas are.

We go to another room to taste and talk further. Nikka divides its malt styles into various flavour groupings, each of which could also be a blend of different styles. The tasting is a chance to see Yoichi from a blender's perspective. Three styles, correct? Sakuma smiles. 'Actually, we make more.' I knew it.

Woody & Vanillic, here as a 12-year-old, is based on lightly peated malt, aged in virgin oak hogsheads and puncheons. It's a glass of tropical fruits, but with Yoichi's burly, oily elegance helping to balance the impact of new oak – though its pine resin and cedar notes are there alongside the aforementioned vanilla. It has the clarity and intensity that mark it as Japanese. 'This fruitiness is a key element in blending,' says Sakuma.

Then comes Sherry & Sweet, again at 12 years old, and also based on lightly peated malt. Here the smoke comes through, alongside almond-like amontillado elements and dried fruit, but Yoichi's heady oiliness, now honey-like, adds a sweetness to the savoury elements from the cask. It's supple, oily, with miso-like depth.

That oiliness gives Yoichi a different physicality to other Japanese whiskies. It lurks, sometimes dangerous, sometimes soothing and restful. How important is texture, I ask Sakuma?

'Each distillery has its own style: sometimes thick, sometimes fruity.

Tadashi Sakuma, the innovator behind Nikka's whiskies.

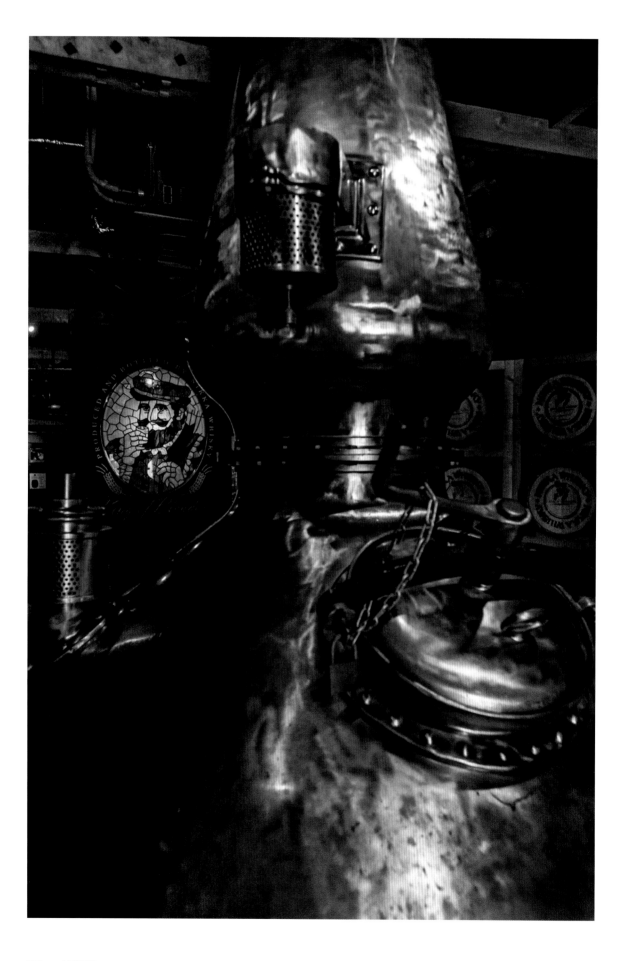

So when we are evaluating or blending, we don't just nose; we taste to find out that texture. Nosing is important, but whisky is a drink!'

We're working up to the big one. Peaty & Salty is what many malt-drinkers think of as Yoichi, although the single malts are in fact blends of many different elements. This comes from heavy peat with some light blended in, and is aged predominantly in casks with lower wood impact: recharred, remade or refill, though there's also a judicious splash of new wood.

It's rich and powerful again, with notes of wintergreen, waxed leather, fur coats and the soy element you normally get from ex-sherry casks. The palate is all smoke and coal dust, mint, the smell of a new drum, spice and pepper.

Here is Yoichi making its most overt homage to Scotland. There's something of Ardbeg in there, but it nods more towards the complexities of Campbeltown's Springbank. And yet there is nothing in Scotland that has the same oiliness, or fruits, or intense lift.

'This is a small selection,' says Sakuma. 'We're making peaty, sherry, fruity, malty — yes, cloudy wort is used sometimes – and woody. Then there's the peating level, the ages and the different casks. And then we can blend.' He grins. 'It's quite complicated.'

How do you define these flavours as being Japanese? 'Scotch remains our master,' he replies. 'That is the way that Taketsuru taught. Then his long life, his personality and his palate all influenced the whiskies he made. He didn't set out to make "Japanese" whisky. What he always wanted to make was his own whisky, and that was the style which evolved. Everything we make still comes from that vision.

'It is made in the grouping of "Scotch type", but we make different styles in a single distillery; we use different yeasts and experiment with other aspects. All the time we are looking to create these different characters. Finally, we are in Japan! The climate is different. All of it gives our character.'

I think of the two men who founded the industry: Torii, with his cleaving to site, and Sen no Rikyu-esque principles; Taketsuru, with his respect for his teachers (there's that Japanese approach to craft) who happened to be in Scotland. Undoubtedly, initially he tried to make what they had shown him. In the wilds of Hokkaido, however, he found his own palate, his own mind, and the conditions took him off that well-trodden path and into something new. Japan and its conditions intervened.

The impact of the distillery's virtual mothballing and the 'Massan effect' resulted in Nikka withdrawing all of its age-statement whiskies (see page 232 for fuller details). The Yoichi range was replaced by a single No Age Statement (NAS) brand.

TASTING NOTES

Aged in a wide range of casks, Yoichi single malt whisky is highly complex.

Yoichi Single Malt (45% ABV) might come as a surprise to some of the distillery's older followers. The smoke has been dialled down as have the sherry casks, though there is a whisper of their dried-fruited dark art on the nose, along with a hazelnut element. The palate is lightly peated, but this is Yoichi relaxing in the summer sun rather than howling at the winter storms. The smoke peeks out a little on the palate along with the distillery's oiliness, which stops it becoming a gentle, sweet, soft whisky.

While the age statements are no longer sold, some may pop up in obscure stores, auction sites, or bars. I would recommend you take a look at the **15-year-old** (45% ABV), which for me showcases the distillery's multifarious characters. Dense, oily with clove, eucalyptus and a salty edge, it slowly opens into smoke, cigar box and walnut. The **20-year-old** (45% ABV) is even smokier, with more of a linseed oil element.

Nikka did bottle numerous single casks and vintage bottlings of Yoichi. As I write, there is a **1988 (bottled 2008 at 55% ABV)** close by. It's all sherry, crystallized ginger, marmalade and smoke with black olive and old leather. It's one of those whiskies that can be used as a tincture – which is just as well, as it's my last bottle.

Actually, one age-statement malt was retained. **Taketsuru 17-year-old** (43% ABV). This is a vatted (or blended) malt using whiskies from Nikka's two malt distilleries and it is a demonstration both of the blender's art and the complexity of those components. Nikka's style might be bolder than Suntory's but it still retains that very Japanese fragrance and intense aromatic profile. Here you get Seville orange, prune, sultana and some quince paste alongside that cigar note that seems to be a house style. Some light vanilla smooths out the tongue before a mix of tart pomegranate and blackberry come across, ahead of a bitter-chocolate finish.

Sapporo

The water from his distillery spills over the pale, polished granite. I'm looking down to the blue ocean and red roofs from this town of the lost and half-forgotten. I fill the cup again, the water flows, the flowers are fresh in the glass. We pick up a glass of whisky and run it over the grave, and the scent of smoke and fruit fills the air. Even the crows fall silent. 'They are looking after us, we believe,' says Emiko. We bow to Massan and Rita, head back downhill.

That afternoon, I'd run my fingers over his rough brown tweed jacket, touched the books, traced his signature and message of love, picked out the linked bamboo (*take*) and crane (*tsuru*) on the border of the *tatami*. This life they both spent between two worlds. What did he think in those years after her death? Which room did he choose? Floor or armchair, English book or Japanese? Did he hear her fingers on the keys? The house speaks more of the man than the whiskies – here you see the love, the connections, the dual life, the real man behind the myth.

Did he succeed or fail, or is it more subtle than that? Was that initial failure in his mind actually a glorious success? Where would we be if he hadn't had to change, if he had stayed on at Yamazaki and not come to this place?

The intent to make Scotch in Japan altered over time. Of course it did. That's what happens anywhere in the world and more potently here than anywhere else. Everything that comes to Japan is changed. Utterly. It could never be the same; the climate, the mindset, the culture will all impact.

That evening, we dine on marbled beef, sipping on glasses of Yoichi, then go to the incredibly dark Bar Ikkei. The bartender is delighted to show off the stock of old Nikka obscurities – vermouth? 3-D labels? Gold & Gold, Da-te, Connexion (a blend of Canadian and Japanese whiskies) – 'That was one of the first ones I did,' says Sakuma – Super Session, a 'Triad blended Whisky' of rye, malt and Coffey grain; and looking like some 1970s cleaning product, Yz; then No Side 900, Nikka's response to Q1000; and News (see page 95). What was the strategy? I ask. 'There wasn't one!' Emiko laughs. 'In the mid-1970s it was "sell as much whisky as much as you can". Then to try everything to get people interested.'

An industry searching again for new ways, for direction. After the pain-free years when everyone wanted it, there was panic and then, finally, it was the calm heart of old principles that saved them, following the geese north once more to Hokkaido. Back, to contemplate and create.

Miyagikyo

宮城峡蒸溜所

Sapporo to Sendai

It was a brief trip to Hokkaido. One day I'll explore it properly – hopefully next time to visit Akkeshi (see page 108) so I can see the east coast. Now, though, we are being drawn back south. Fly to Sendai, bus to Miyagikyo, back to Sendai, *shinkansen* back to Tokyo – then home.

Suddenly, it's the last day. Take and I have been so caught up in this bubble that the road seemed to be stretching on forever. The trip had become our life: train, plane, car, distillery, shrine, water, mountains. As we travel, news has been coming in of new distilleries being planned and setting up. We could continue. We have momentum. Not now, though.

We meet the BBC crew at the airport, struggling with kit and slightly recalcitrant check-in staff. They're heading to Tasmania to see what is happening at another of whisky's new frontiers. It will have its own founding myths, teething problems and slow development of style. Its geography will impact, as will wine culture and the needs of the Aussie whisky-drinker. Another chapter opens. Blank pages to be filled. Footprints to be made.

The transfers all work, and we head west from Sendai to the distillery, the city dribbling out into light industrial estates and then countryside. Imper-

ceptibly, the mountains begin to dictate the road's direction. Signs for *onsen* begin to appear. Those sharp, raw ridges, the conical peaks, forest-clad, point to the seethe and bubble under the surface. In autumn, the colours seem to reflect the rising lava lake beneath, hot reds and ochres, burnt umber.

Every trip I've made to Miyagikyo has been slightly different. Mostly done in a day, new aspects of the complexity of the site revealed in each one – you never get it all on the first visit. The clouds are low again, less of the foggy mountains that Take likes, more just fog. The distillery site is on a wedge of land between the Nikkawa and Hirose rivers. We go in search of the joining of the waters, where the rivers meet. It's too far away for a photo.

We turn back and head to the pebble beach close to the distillery where, legend has it, Taketsuru tasted the water and declared it good. The first distillation was put into the waters as thanks. We sip, then turn back towards the distillery. I slip a river-rounded pebble in my pocket, thinking of Suzuki and time.

A farewell to Hokkaido.

MIYAGIKYO

Miyagikyo, with its wide main road and tall red buildings, has the air of a newly built midwestern American city. Its size speaks of its time. Here was Nikka in 1969 reacting boldly to the growth of the domestic market. 'The earliest idea was that it would be one-and-a-half-times bigger than Yoichi,' chief blender Tadashi Sakuma explains. 'Then we expanded it further with the grain distillery, which arrived here in 1999. Now it's three times larger than Yoichi.' This makes Miyagikyo one of three Japanese distilleries that make grain and malt on the same site.

The search for an appropriate site took three years, before Taketsuru's seal of approval on the riverbank. As Taketsuru opined, the humidity created from this watery convergence would produce a specific microclimate suitable for maturation. The flat plain was also large enough to build a substantial plant with room for further expansion, which happened in 1979, and again a decade later. It certainly made more commercial sense, with better communication links to the major markets.

The distillery's buildings are separated by mini-plantations of trees and bushes that circle a large ornamental lake at the site's centre. At times you feel as if you are walking in a park rather than round a working site.

Miyagikyo is also, these days, as well known for its grain as it is for its single malt. If Yoichi helped to bust open the notion of Japanese single malt, then this distillery's Coffey Grain and Coffey Malt made single-malt lovers realize (finally) that grain wasn't neutral packing spirit, but filled with character.

I recall being here once with a group of Swedish whisky nuts, malt-whisky purists to a man. After an extensive tasting, the only whisky every one of them bought was grain. Another small victory. Coffey Grain didn't just open up another area for Japanese whisky; it helped to shift the debate about grain whisky globally.

Inside, the stillhouse has the usual slightly confusing truncated view of stills that stretch upwards to an unseen point. All that's in front of me is a name plate: 'Blair's Glasgow, 1963'. A similar plate, dated two years after, is on the other still.

Miyagikyo's kiln rears into the sky.

宮城峡蒸溜所

Blair, Campbell & McLean started trading in 1838. Closely involved in fabricating sugar machinery, it branched into still-making later that century. Based in Govan, Glasgow, the company ceased trading in 1977.

The two stills are of the design patented by Aeneas Coffey in 1832, which ushered in the era of grain whisky. When Taketsuru studied in Scotland, he spent a period at the (now-defunct) Bo'ness distillery near Edinburgh, studying Coffey-still distillation. The fact that he chose this design over the others available in 1969, when the technology had moved on, reinforces his continued adherence to tradition.

Coffey stills consist of two linked columns: an analyzer and a rectifier. The wash is stripped of alcohol in the former and the vapour diverted into the rectifier. This column is divided into a series of compartments (24 in this case) or 'plates'. As the vapour rises, so the heavier compounds begin to reflux. By the time the vapour reaches the condenser, only the lightest remain. Coffey stills, however, give a richer feel to the spirit that comes through in blends. It's that umami thing again. 'We believe that Coffey stills just give more character. Not only do you get the nature of the raw material, but it is very sweet and richly textured compared to other whiskies,' explains Sakuma.

The stills were originally at Nikka's Nishinomiya plant and came here in the 1999 expansion (the firm has another set at its Tochigi distillery) and now produce a number of styles: 'Five or six,' says Sakuma enigmatically. Two of those are made with a 100% malted barley mash, rather than the normal corn/malt mix. It was this 'Coffey malt' that made the malt-whisky lovers prick up their ears when it was launched as a single-cask release. It is now part of the Nikka core range. Originally, though, it was created as another option for the blends.

'We vary the styles by using different yeasts,' Sakuma explains. 'By collecting the spirit at different plates we get different strengths and styles. We make light, medium, heavy, heavier … and super-heavy!

'We've also experimented with rye. Remember the Super Session from last night [see page 221]? That had some of that rye in it, but we're not working with it at the moment.'

Again, here is this idea that while driving quality forward is a constant, everything else is flexible.

'Flexibility and innovation is the Japanese way,' Sakuma says. 'The Coffey malt is innovative in itself, but we make two different types, then age them in a mix of casks. The Coffey grain is also a blend of more than one style. It is part of the aim to make a good, balanced whisky.

'The grains were something to differentiate Nikka from the rest, but after we launched them, the grain market became noisy. Now they are increasingly important in the global market – especially the bar scene. We are proud to have activated it.' Grain here is a statement.

The same approach applies in the malt distillery. Like Yoichi, the malted barley is blended to different levels of smokiness, though unpeated is the most commonly used type. How many malts? I ask, knowing that the answer will contain some caveat. 'We make unpeated, light peat, malty, and estery, so that's four types.' He pauses. 'Oh, and a secret one.' There are probably more, to be honest. There are two mash tuns (holding nine and six tonnes) the wort from each being kept separate. The fermentation

The two Coffey stills produce the innovative Nikka grain whiskies.

time is shorter than Yoichi – between 48 and 60 hours – while a different set of yeasts to Yoichi, and the grain side, is used.

The stillhouse is divided into two, with each half having two pairs of wash and spirit stills. All are the same size and shape: large, fat with a boil bulb, long neck and upward-angled lyne arms. All of these help to increase reflux and produce a lighter character. Heating is by steam, and condensing is in shell and tube condensers. Everything, in fact, is the opposite of Yoichi.

While the grain is aged at Nikka's Tochigi plant, the malt remains here, maturing in low warehouses in a mix of cask types including ex-Sherry, which also includes an increased amount of recharred American oak casks (barrels, hogsheads and puncheons). We head to the cooperage to see it underway.

After a cask has been filled (and obviously emptied) for a second time, it comes here. The inner carbon layer is scraped off and the interior set on fire. We watch as it smoulders, then the alcohol burns bright blue and sparks begin to rise before the cask ignites, sheets of flames rising, the centre like the rising sun. You expect the whole thing to go up in flames, but after 30 seconds the burner is turned off, water is sprayed in and the aroma of toast, cooked banana, roast almond, chocolate and vanilla rises. 'We'll get another cycle out of it now,' says Sakuma. It is money-saving, but also adds a mid-point flavour between brand-new (virgin) wood and first-fill. Again, it increases the options for blending.

Our tasting follows a similar format to yesterday's at Yoichi, with component parts of the distillery's output rather than the finished product.

The new-make of the medium-weight Coffey grain is sweet and fat with a gently floral element and a palate already thick with creaminess. It will be aged in recharred ex-bourbon hogsheads and refill casks.

Woody & Mellow grain follows, all dreamy butterscotch, caramel, vanilla pods and banana split with added red and tropical fruit. It's only the cooked-corn note that persuades you this isn't rum.

'This is the main base malt for the blends,' says Sakuma pointing to a glass of Malty & Soft single malt. It's more malted milk than dry and nutty – that gently fruited Miyagikyo style coming through. It hits the palate in waltz rhythm: slow, quick-quick, slow.

Fruity & Rich shows more oak, along with rounded and slightly fleshy fruits. Here is Miyagikyo's generous sweet persimmon, baked pineapple and quince, while the American oak adds custard and a dusting of cinnamon over apple sponge. An imaginary blend builds in my head.

Even the use of bolder casks in Sherry & Sweet doesn't diminish the sweetness of the distillery character, though now the fruits have gone from soft and pulpy into ripe blackberries, while the palate mingles molasses with a plummy, honeyed depth. All have this gentle power, this physical thickness. 'It could be the yeast,' says Sakuma. 'as well as giving flavour, it can add texture.'

The range of possibilities here and at Yoichi are needed, not just for blends but for single malts. In 2015, faced with severely depleted stock made worse by the 'Massan effect' (see page 210), Nikka took the decision to withdraw all of its aged-statement whiskies (with the exception

Re-charring casks at Miyagikyo.

宮城峡蒸溜所

Column stills (opposite) and pots (above). Miyagikyo has both.

of Taketsuru 17-year-old) and replace them with No Age Statement [NAS] alternatives.

NAS has become a controversial topic in whisky, but if you have limited stock and rising demand, what else can you do? The only reason for the controversy is that the whisky industry as a whole has either stated or implied that the older a whisky is, the better it will be and therefore age statements can be used as an indicator of quality.

Removing the age statement allows whisky-makers to break this paradigm and allows drinkers to concentrate on flavour rather than numbers. We are right back to Jota Tanaka's 'arc of maturity': a topic that has run through every visit.

All good in theory, but even knowledgeable drinkers ask about age before they taste. If Japanese whisky is to establish a base that will allow it to grow once more at the end of this period of stock-induced stasis, it has to convince sceptical drinkers about the benefits of NAS.

Sakuma's approach is fascinating. 'When I make, say, Miyagikyo 15-year-old, I want to make the perfect example of Miyagikyo at that age: the different styles and wood types reflecting a single point in the whisky's life. Taking an age statement away means I can pick from any point along that timeline – younger whiskies, older ones, different styles and woods. This is a chance for me to be creative, for whisky to be creative. The whiskies I am making should reflect this and be different from, but as good or better than, the ones they are replacing.

'I have the potential to go in many different directions,' he continues. 'Even though we had to discontinue age statements there is an opportunity to increase the range, because age is simply one aspect of style. We should turn this situation into a new opportunity, but first we have to change the mindset about age.

'This is a good opportunity to change the world because we can create so many different types of whisky. We've already had success with the new range, with the two Coffey Grains and Nikka From The Barrel. I want to to expand this innovative approach – I want to promote a new experience.' Out of crisis comes opportunity.

Is this another manifestation of the Japanese willingness to change, while still being traditional? He nods. 'Basically, Japanese people try to adhere to their own style and always try to improve to achieve better results. That innovation starts with tradition. Thanks to the heritage of the founders, we have tangible and intangible assets that allow us to develop new things with no restrictions.'

It comes from the past, it is within the DNA: the intense, clear style; awareness of palate; belief in repetition and importance of tiny details; the constant improvement while remaining within the tradition of the craft.

We can mourn the passing of the age statements, but in all honesty, what was the alternative? Retain them and restrict sales, or be bold and, while risking the wrath of whisky-drinkers, ensure that as many people as possible could enjoy the drink?

NAS is a hotly debated topic in whisky and Sakuma's belief in how they can liberate a whisky-maker and issue in new possibilities is a welcome and calmly rational addition to the debate. It's clear from continuing our chat that Nikka's approach to NAS is not going to be restricted to one expression. Getting rid of the fetters of age statements could be the most exciting development yet.

In terms of bottled product, these days the major focus at Miyagikyo is on the two Coffey-still grain whiskies. The **Coffey Grain** (45% ABV) is the softer of the two, but will be a wake-up call for those who think of grain whisky as being gossamer-thin. This has rich corn-cob sweetness alongside toffee apple, some black grapes, honey and a back note of anise and sumac before some orange zest livens things up and a scent like a freshly sharpened pencil announces that there's oak in here as well. It's sweet, rich and rounded, while with water more *onsen*/sauna notes emerge. The palate is all orange-blossom honey and in typical Coffey-still style it clings to the tongue like a tin of peaches.

The **Coffey Malt** (45% ABV) is as rich, but also drier, with more chocolate and cherry, hard caramel and a roasted element that adds a certain seriousness to proceedings. The palate is slightly less eager to please than the Coffey Grain, which comes across like an enthusiastic Labrador puppy. There's sweetness but also a clear nutty, oaken frame along with golden syrup and baked peaches. Complex and smooth.

The new **Miyagikyo Single Malt** (43% ABV) is a seamless continuation of the now-culled age statements. It opens with almost Cognac-like fruitiness with flowers, fruits and a red-apple element. Lush and soft, there's persimmon and a palate-coating effect of melting milk chocolate and mocha. A slightly bready note adds just a hint of dryness. All of Miyagikyo's quiet sweetness is on show: baked apple, a light mintiness, some nougat, and just a scintilla of smoke.

As with Yoichi, there could be bottles of this lurking behind bars. If you chance upon one, please do try it; and if you track down the **15-year-old** (45% ABV) you will have what was for me the best of the bunch: all sweet persimmon and toffee with some honey and just a hint of piney oak.

Grain whiskies are key to Nikka's strategy.

Sendai to Tokyo

The rain is on again, slowing the traffic down as we make our way back to Sendai. 'We've missed our train.' Emiko doesn't seem too concerned. 'It's OK. There's a *shinkansen* every hour. We can have something to eat.' Now you're talking. We're in Sendai where the 'something' actually means only one thing—tongue! Specifically, *gyūtan*, thin slices of beef tongue grilled rapidly over charcoal. Naturally, there's a choice of establishments at the station. I'm so going to miss this when I get back home and am forced to chose between insipid baguettes, potentially hazardous sushi and entero-disastrous burritos. You can't get a decent Highball either. You can here, so we did. Everyone is relaxing. We joke and toast the end of the trip, making plans for our next meeting on the neverending global whisky tour, then sleep all the way back to Tokyo.

When in Sendai, there is only one thing to eat – *gyūtan*.

WATER

Water had been following me and I don't mean just falling from the sky. It flowed in rivers and springs, it fixed distilleries' sites, cascaded in sacred water-falls and out of spouts at shrines where we washed our hands and mouths. You needed water to dye, to make *washi* and ceramics. More than that, it was the basis of the tea ceremony, the heart of cooking.

'Kyoto cuisine is a cuisine of water,' chef Hashimoto had told me in Kyoto. 'When we offer *dashi* at the start of a meal it is to show the purity of the water.' It had reminded me of a conversation with another Michelin-starred chef, Hal Yamashita, whose restaurant in Tokyo specializes in ingredients from his home in Kobe – including water, which is shipped from there three times a week. 'Water is the most important part of cooking,' he told me. 'I am making Kobe-style food. To do that properly I have to bring in Kobe water. The water here in Tokyo is totally different.'

I recalled Jota and Take's talk of the 'spiritual' soba taken only with water, or the reverence for ice in bars. Everywhere there was water.

What, then, of whisky? The source needs to be pure, the water must be there in volume and at the right temperature for condensing. As Kenny Gray, an old Scottish distilling friend, once told me, 'All we do is move water, Dave. We add it in malting, then we take it away. We add it again in mashing, then we take it away again in distilling. We add some to the cask, then in the bottle and then in the glass. Water-carriers, that's all we are.'

Does its quality make a difference to flavour? Most distillers feel it doesn't, but not all. Ichiro Akuto's family transported Chichibu water 60km (37 miles) to their distillery at Hanyu because they felt it helped with quality.

Shinji Fukuyo is also on the side of the believers. 'As an experiment we used Hakushu water at Yamazaki and the spirit was different. We don't know why. We can't find any correlation between the mineral content and flavour, but it's a fact as far as I am concerned. Different waters make their own character.'

Water is central to Japanese craft.

ZEN

I had been leery about drawing comparisons between Zen and whisky – actually, Zen and anything. It seems too lazy. And yet, in every book I read, every conversation I had, there it was, influencing, shaping the flow. It was never overt, but discreet, there and not-there, which is very Zen.

On a previous trip I had spent time in the Shunko-in temple in Kyoto with deputy abbot Takafumi Kawakami, the fourth generation of his family to teach here. 'My purpose here is to teach that Buddhist practice is in our life's activities,' he told me. 'This is a temple for people who want to come and learn to sit *zazen*. It is getting back to basics, and Zen's idea is getting back to basics.

'That means learning through experience. Sitting is empirical study. It trains you to live in the now, because by the time you have read this, that "now" has gone and is in the past. By living in the now you create a perfect past.'

Before staying at the temple I was falling into the trap of using whisky as a metaphor for Zen: distillation as concentration; the purification of the spirit as being like that of the mind; or perhaps how the murky clouds of wash are transformed into something clean and infinitely more powerful. Hey, it's just like the mind! It all sounded pretty good, until I sat at Shunko-in and realized that it's all rubbish. Whisky is whisky.

As if to drum it home, after the session, while reading a book of teachings by Nyogen Senzaki, this passage leapt out: 'If I serve you a cup of tea and say this is a symbol of Zen none of you … will enjoy such a lukewarm beverage…Why? Because the sipping is the appreciation and the appreciation is the sipping. Zen never says "try this and you will be enlightened". It only demands the action which is enlightenment itself.'

As Rev. Kawakami said to me, whisky isn't really compatible with Zen – this is about keeping the mind clear, after all. Neither is it an aid to creativity. How many times have we all had that moment of realization after the fifth dram when the cure to the problems of the world appears with astonishing clarity? We write the answer down, but when we discover the paper the next morning we can't read our own writing.

And yet, the framework that helped to establish the Japanese approach to craftsmanship is embedded in the arrival of Zen. As Carol Steinberg Gould and Mara Miller (*Japanese Aesthetics*, www.aesthetics-on-line.org) wrote: 'Zen Buddhism is at the heart of what

many ... consider distinctive to the Japanese aesthetic: suggestiveness, irregularity, asymmetry, simplicity, and perishability.' It is, I believe, an impulse at the core of the Japanese approach to whisky as well.

Meditating on 'whisky' does, however, bring a greater understanding of the interdependent nature of the whisky-making process, not just the physical creation of the drink, but the wider world that brings in the now and the past: the place where it was born and its environment, the ingredients, the people involved. With one sip you are entering into this web of linked happenings. The aroma and taste are in themselves a complex weaving together of molecules acting in accord with each other. Nothing in that glass – and by extension anywhere – exists in isolation.

You need an open mind to taste well. Understanding aroma is a matter of being actively engaged with the world. The aroma of a complex whisky can help with that engagement. That engagement – being aware of the complexities of smells that always swirl around you – helps with the whisky.

Can whisky be a metaphor for Zen?

Tokyo

'Just one drink,' I say to Take as we get out at Tokyo Station. He needs to get back to his family, I need to pack. We head into Shimbashi's backstreets once again, grab a cold one in one of the old beer joints. 'Maybe some food?' he says. 'Just one plate.' Whisky is off the menu; tonight is a night for sake. We find one of those strange underground food dens packed with restaurants, locate a promising-looking establishment where cup after cup of what seems to be increasingly amazing *nihonshu* begin to appear, accompanied by more than one plate.

The conversation is fast, one of the slightly manic and rushed ones you have on last nights, as if everything that you'd meant to say for the past three weeks has suddenly been remembered. We laugh at the memories, clink cups. 'You: home,' I say. 'Your family needs you.' He has been mentor, accomplice, teacher and most of all friend, but it's the nature of our peripatetic lives that meetings are intense and brief. This project has already lasted longer than most. I watch him go and head back to the comfort of the Park Hotel. Bow at the shrine at the corner. You never know.

A lot of time has passed, yet somehow now it all seems rushed. There's a case to unpack and repack with the stuff that had been left in storage, presents to cram into nooks, bottles to wrap in T-shirts. Eventually it's stuffed and, after some encouragement, shut. I'm on the early-morning flight from Haneda. It's pointless going to bed now. I sit and watch the dawn gild the towers once more, go downstairs and head to the airport.

There's always time for one last drink.

KAIZEN

And so they get up the next day, the *shokunin*, the furnace-master, potter, *washi*-maker, woodworker, and the barman, chef, metalworker, tea-maker, printer, weaver, incense-listener, the blenders and the distillers. Somewhere, someone is nosing a glass, another tuning in to the song of steam; in the hills one is hunting for *mizunara* in the dense, dripping wood.

Today, they will do their jobs again, but try to do them better. They believe in *kaizen*, and the ethos of quality through forensic attention to detail. It's repetition that is never repetitive, but always moving forward. They pour themselves into the things they create: the cocktail, the piece of fish, the cup of tea, the new-make and blend.

Whisky, we are told, is about consistency: making the same thing each day to ensure that the identity of that distillery sings, that the blend will remain the same. Yet by solely obsessing on consistency, tradition atrophies. That is no way for a craft already under pressure to grow. Consistency should never be used as a way to hamper improvements, or thwart innovation. That is why *kaizen* is so important within Japanese whisky-making – more important than the consistency some international colleagues say is their top priority.

The *shokunin* approach brings the maker closer to the made; the aim is to see the essence of the clay, or the tealeaf, or the weird complexities achieved with grain, yeast, water, and wood interacting with specific conditions.

Chef Hal Yamashita said to me once, 'The Japanese approach to cooking is very different to that of the West. That is based on adding flavours to a base ingredient. Here we take things away so as not to interfere with the ingredients' flavours, but to enhance them. It means I have to be able to understand the ingredients completely.'

That philosophy applies across all crafts. In whisky it means paying attention to aroma, flavour and texture; it means simplicity, it means transparency. There is nowhere to hide. The pool is clear. It has *shibui*.

All of the *shokunin* I met spoke of this, but all also emphasized the need to be open to chance because creativity cannot be controlled or planned; it is wild and unpredictable.

Distillation is controlled, its parameters set. Then the spirit is put into cask and chance enters the equation. It's like putting clay in the kiln, or Horiki's dyeing of *washi*. A whisky-maker will know the likely outcome

of this distillate in this type of wood for this length of time, but none can say exactly what will happen. Two casks of the same age from the same tree, filled on the same day with the same spirit will produce two different results.

It's those surprises that help push whisky forward. It's Cohen's 'cracks in everything' again; irregularity, assymetry. It lies in a willingness to open up to natural and unknown processes in order to make the drink expressive and compelling. Whisky-making is crafts-manship.

All of Japan's crafts were washed up on its shores, then turned into something that was its own, moulded by time and climate, hand and season, philosophy and war, poverty and richness of heart, by perseverance, isolation and openness.

It is why they make the best Japanese whisky in the world.

Gassho!

Craft is controlled, steady, yet wild and innovative.

Glossary

Chawan: Teaware.

Chibidaru: Literally, cute casks.

Chinquapin: Species of oak.

Dashi: Stock for soba noodles. Traditionally made from water, kombu seaweed and bonito (tuna-like fish flakes).

Dogū: Clay figures from the Jomon era.

Gaijin: Foreigner.

Gassho: 'Palms together', giving thanks.

Gyūtan: Grilled beef tongue.

Haiku: A traditional three-line poem.

Hashiri: The start of a new season.

Heain era: 794–1185.

Hinoki: Japanese cypress used in construction and incense.

Hoiro: Table used in the drying of tea.

Ichi-go ichi-e: One time, one meeting, one encounter.

Izakaya: Informal bar-restaurant.

Jotan: Paper on which tea is rolled.

Kaiseke: High-end formal cuisine. A speciality of Kyoto.

Kanji: Chinese ideograms.

Kaizen: Continual incremental improvement.

Kami: Paper.

Kawaii: Cuteness.

Kegani: Hairy crab.

Kigo: Words associated with a specific season used in haiku poetry.

Koji: *Aspergillus oryzae*, fungus used to initiate fermentation in sake, *shōchū*, miso, soy sauce.

Kombu: Kelp used in the making of *dashi*.

Maiko: Geisha in Kyoto dialect.

Mizunara: *Quercus crispula* (aka Japanese oak).

Mizuwari: A drink – whisky, ice and water.

Nagori: The end of a season.

Nattō: Fermented soy beans held together by slimy mucilaginous threads. An acquired taste.

Negiyaki: Pancakes with spring onions.

Nihonshu: Sake.

Okonomiyaki: A kind of pancake.

Onigiri: Rice balls.

Onsen: A hot-spring bath.

Ryokan: Traditional inn.

Sakura: Cherry blossom.

Sanshō: Japanese term for Sichuan 'pepper' (actually a member of the citrus/rue family).

Sekki: Collective term for the 24 'small seasons'.

Shinkansen: Bullet train.

Shokunin: Master craftsman.

Shun: The peak of the season.

Sudachi: A type of Japanese citrus. It has similarities to lime and green yuzu.

Tanuki: Raccoon dog.

Tatami: Floor mat.

Temomi: Hand-rolling (of tea).

Torii: A gate, often at the entrance to a shrine.

Tsukemono: Collective term for Japanese pickles.

Udon: Thick wheat noodles.

Ukiyo-e: Woodblock prints.

Umami: The fifth taste, stimulated by glutamic acid.

Wabi-cha: Rustic tea.

Washi: Mulberry-pulp paper.

Yakitori: Charcoal-grilled skewers of meat and vegetable.

Zazen: Seated meditation.

Bibliography

Basho, Matsuo, *The Narrow Road to the Deep North* (London, 1966)

Black, John R., *Young Japan* (replica edition, London, 2005)

Bunting, Chris, *Drinking Japan* (North Clarendon, VT, 2011)

Checkland, Olive, *Japanese Whisky, Scotch Blend* (Edinburgh, 1998)

Dōgen (ed. Kazuaki Tanahashi), *Moon in a Dewdrop* (New York, NY, 1985)

Durston, Diane, *Old Kyoto: A Guide to Traditional Shops, Restaurants and Inns* (New York, NY, 2013)

Goulding, Matt, *Rice, Noodle, Fish* (London, 2015)

Hearn, Lafcadio, *Writings from Japan: An Anthology* (London, 1984)

Horiki, Eriko, *Architectural Spaces with Washi* (Tokyo, 2007)

Horiki, Eriko, *Washi in Architecture* (Menorca, Spain, 2006)

Iyer, Pico, *The Lady and the Monk* (London, 1991)

Kerr, Alex, *Lost Japan* (London, 2015)

Koren, Leonard, *Wabi-Sabi: for Artists, Designers, Poets and Philosophers* (Berkeley, CA, 1994)

Koren, Leonard, *Wabi-Sabi: Further Thoughts* (Point Reyes, CA, 2015)

Leach, Bernard, *A Potter in Japan* (London, 2015)

McKinsey & Co (eds), *Reimagining Japan: The Quest for a Future That Works* (San Francisco, CA, 2010)

Okakura, Kakuzo, *The Book of Tea* (print on demand, via amazon.co.uk)

Ono, Sokyo, *Shinto the Kami Way* (North Clarendon VT, 1976)

Phillipi, Donald L., *Songs of Gods, Songs of Humans* (Princeton, NJ, 1979)

Richie, Donald (ed. Arturo Silva), *The Donald Richie Reader* (Berkeley, CA, 2005)

Richie, Donald, *A Tractate on Japanese Aesthetics* (Berkeley, CA, 2007)

Sadler, A.L., *The Japanese Tea Ceremony* (North Clarendon, VT, 2008)

Sakaki, Nanao, *Break the Mirror* (Berkeley CA, 1987)

Senzaki, Nyogen, *Eloquent Silence* (Somerville, MA, 2008)

Scherer, James, *The Romance of Japan* (London, 1935)

Shirane, Haruo, *Japan and the Culture of the Four Seasons* (New York, NY, 2013)

Snyder, Gary, *The Practice of the Wild* (San Francisco, CA, 1990)

Tanizaki, Junichiro, *In Praise of Shadows* (London, 2001)

Yanagi, Soetsu, *The Unknown Craftsman* (New York, NY, 2103)

Yonemoto, Marcia, *Mapping Early Modern Japan* (Berkeley, CA, 2003)

Waley, Arthur, *The Noh Plays of Japan* (North Clarendon, VT, 1976)

Index

About the Author

Dave Broom has been writing about whisky for 25 years. He is the author of eight books, two of which (*Drink!* and *Rum*) won the Glenfiddich Award for Drinks Book of the Year. He has also won the Glenfiddich Award for Drinks Writer of the Year twice and recently won the prestigious IWSC Communicator of the Year Award. In 2015, *Tales of the Cocktail* presented Dave with the Best Cocktail & Spirits award, soon to be followed by the Golden Spirit Award in 2016.

Over his two decades in the field, Dave has built up a considerable international following with regular training/educational visits to France, Holland, Germany, the USA and Japan. His remit has covered consumer features as well as business reports. He is also actively involved in whisky education, acting as a consultant to major distillers on tasting techniques as well as teaching professionals and the public. He was also one of the developers of Diageo's generic whisky tasting tool, the Flavour Map™.

Acknowledgements

This book would not have been possible without the help of the following people.

In Japan, Jota Tanaka, Shiho Shimizu, Koki Takehira, Mike Miyamoto, Ichiro Akuto, Yumi Yoshikawa, Manami Momma, Hisashi Maemura, Hiyashi Kishi, Takayuki Suzuki, Atsushi Horigami, Eriko Horiki, Shinki Yamashita, Chef Kenichi Hashimoto, Genpei Yamanaka, Kotaru Sakai, Yusuke Matsubayashi, Mikio Hiraishi, Emiko Kaji, Tadashi Sakuma, and everyone at all the distilleries. Thank you for your patience and wisdom.

A particular thank you to Shinji Fukuyo for all the help, kindness and friendship over the years which has helped me along the road to some understanding.

There are hundreds of people who have assisted me over the years in trying to deepen my understanding of Japan and its whiskies. I have been particularly indebted to Dr Shigeo Sato, Mas Minabi (who taught me about transparency on my first day), Seiichi Koshimizu, Dr Koichi Inatomi, Keita Minari, and Takahiro Itoga. Sadly, one of my great mentors, Naofumi Kamiguchi passed away soon after the book was finished. His constant good humour and passion for the whiskies of Nikka helped light fires of understanding the world over.

A bow to the host of bartenders I have sat and watched, listened to and sipped in front of. There have been many and sadly there isn't the space to thank you all here. Please know that I appreciate your wisdom, skill, and love for great drinks. Thank you especially to Hidetsugu Ueno who has acted as a focal point for the world's best on their visits to Tokyo, and to Tatsuya Minagawa for bringing his knowledge to Scotland.

To fellow (and better) writers Chris Bunting for his belief in setting up Nonjatta – which shouid be everyone's first port of call for information about Japanese whisky – and Stefan van Eyken for carrying on the great work. To Nick Coldicott – good luck with the sake! – and to Rob Allanson and Dom Roskrow for indulging me as I started to write about this subject.

To all at Treeleaf Zendo and Rev. Takafumi Kawakami.

Once again, I've been supported by the amazing team at Octopus: Denise Bates bought into the idea from the off and allowed me to pursue this slightly different course, to Juliette Norsworthy for design, Katherine Hockley for production, the unflappable Alex Stetter for editing, and Margaret Rand and Jamie Ambrose for assiduous reading. And my agent Tom Williams for helping to nurture the idea and giving me the confidence to carry it through.

To Yuki Yamazaki for company, drams, translating skills, bitters, and sheer infectious enthusiasm for life. To all at whisk-E over the years who have become true friends: Yoichi, Toshi, Maki, Kimi, and Ogachi, our driver.

To Marcin Miller, the drunken monkey, for sending me to Japan for the first time and being a sounding board, confidant, travelling companion and most of all friend. Couldn't have done it without you.

To my fellow road warrior Kohei Take not just for his superlative images but for understanding this quest from the outset and helping this clumsy gaijin in so many ways. He joined as a photographer, but ended as a true friend. This has been a truly collaborative effort. With special thanks to Alice Lascelles and Alicia Kirby for helping to bring us together

To my wife Jo, who for almost two decades has put up with me heading off to the east and then listening to my raves and rants, ideas. She's coped with writerly moods, filed bottles, kept things in order. I love you, and to my darling daughter Rosie, whose love of Japan seems to grow with every day. I promise you will both come there with me.

Most of all, to David Croll and Noriko Kakuda whose amazing generosity, friendship, insider knowledge, patience, and trust has deepened my love of Japan. I cannot repay the debt I owe you both, but perhaps the dedicating of this small offering to you both will give a small indication of how much I love you.

Arigato gozaimasu!